# CONNECT FOUR

*"One woman's journey of fear, love, connection, and vulnerability to reinvent herself"*

MELISSA BREVIC

authorHOUSE®

*AuthorHouse™*
*1663 Liberty Drive*
*Bloomington, IN 47403*
*www.authorhouse.com*
*Phone: 1 (800) 839-8640*

*Published by AuthorHouse 08/19/2019*

*ISBN: 978-1-7283-2326-8 (sc)*
*ISBN: 978-1-7283-2324-4 (hc)*
*ISBN: 978-1-7283-2325-1 (e)*

*Library of Congress Control Number: 2019912171*

*Print information available on the last page.*

*Any people depicted in stock imagery provided by Getty Images are models, and such images are being used for illustrative purposes only. Certain stock imagery © Getty Images.*

*This book is printed on acid-free paper.*

# Introduction

Today is day one of my sabbatical. I took this reprieve from teaching to work towards a second master's degree in education. I received my first master's in Educational Leadership a decade ago, so it has been a long time since I wrote a paper or read educational literature. However, I am ready and prepared with motivation, perseverance, and purpose.

Day one is quiet. Lonely, but oh, so liberating. It has been years since I have been alone. Truly alone. Now since both of my sons are in school full-time, the liberation of time and space present themselves — something novel and unusual —time for me.

The freedom of time has inspired me to write. I intend to write through a stream of consciousness that has accumulated and filled my heart and soul for years. Woven through my words will be four themes: joy, connection, love, and empathy. Sometimes these themes will be expressed from my experiences, and sometimes they will be embedded in the love and support I received from the people with whom I surround myself. At times, the experiences of others shared and trusted with me will be tucked into my stories.

Like the strategies utilized in the class game, *Connect Four*, the four pervasive themes intertwined in my stories mandate moments of pause, reflection, and decision-making. In these moments, strategies emerge. *What is my next move? What if I can't place my "checker" there? What if my projected progress gets blocked?* These reflections and strategies can create fear and anxiety, but they can also create motivation, excitement, and joy.

Similarly, throughout my vignettes of life, strategies are employed to achieve happiness, discovery, and accomplishment. Paired with making "connections," I doggedly ensure that I combat fear and generate joy, connection, love, and empathy. Ultimately, fear is decimated and overtaken by the "four in a row." These themes, coupled with positive and healthy relationships, arm me with strategies to ensure a happy life and the best version of myself.

I look forward to the catharsis of release and sharing the prevalent four themes with my readers. Though I have no idea what emotions will emerge, I will embrace the unexpected stops along my bumpy and careening journey, but most importantly, I anticipate developing many meaningful connections with my readers.

I wish for you to take away one shred of hope, a beacon of light, or a simple word or phrase that resonates with you. I hope you connect with me on my journey and find a deep part of yourself that has been stifled or idle in your subconscious. I want you along with me on this journey. After all, it is through personal connections that relationships are built, nurtured, and maintained.

Before we travel to my childhood, I must explain the crowning of the "mom of goats."

~

# Crowned

I have two sons: Brady, who is eight, and Cody, who is six. They are my entire world, but they are exhausting. They are typical boys; full of energy, competition, and dirt — literally and figuratively. They are rough and tough. They enjoy wrestling, fighting, and turning into chameleons for whatever sport is in season. Most days, they are covered in grime, and I cringe at the sight of their dirt-clad shoes and socks, but I remind myself often that without them, I would feel alone. Not the alone I am currently enjoying, but the kind of deep void that only my sons could fill.

As with most young girls, I drafted the quintessential journey in my mind: get married at twenty-three to a handsome man with a dynamic personality, have three kids (two girls and a boy), before the age of thirty and live in a beautiful home with a wrap-around porch. Though some of these dreams manifested (my husband is handsome and dynamic), most were just that: dreams. As my mother-in-law would say, "Man plans — God laughs."

My husband, Scott, and I married on July 27, 2002. I was twenty-seven, which meant already my childhood dream had evaporated because in my warped mind I thought that twenty-seven was too old to get married, but after accepting my age, I was ready to enjoy the married life. Scott and I immediately loved our life together. We traveled a lot, threw fun get-togethers, and capitalized on our time alone.

However, it wasn't long before I received the *baby itch*. Again, I had a timeline. I needed babies before thirty. *It had to happen.* The script was written, and it was time for it to manifest. Our ignorance, however, blinded us to the idea that the only thing standing in our way of becoming parents was reality. We were ignorant to the possibility of having trouble when trying to conceive, but even once we accepted it, no one could have prepared us for the obstacles that reality had in store.

After traveling for a few years to various exquisite destinations —Las Vegas, Jamaica, St. Lucia, Sonoma, Napa, and the Bahamas, we were ready. Getting pregnant seemed a given. If you wanted a baby, it was done. Baby made. I vividly remember traveling to the Bahamas knowing this was the time. Butterflies danced in my stomach, visions swirled in my head, and my belly seemed alive with the potential of a baby residing in it. In my mind, I would always remember the Bahamas and the opportunity it provided to make me a mother.

I wasn't prepared, however, to accept the disappointments. The rejections. The pain. The suffering. The endless trips to CVS to purchase a pregnancy test only to find out it is negative once again. No one prepares you for the magnitude of your wedding vows: "*in sickness and in health, in good times and in bad.*" No one reminds you that love will be tested. Truly tested. No one preaches that your partner needs to be resilient and willing to stick through the rough terrain with you and that marriage must exemplify unconditional love.

For years, we experienced all of it. Disappointments. Rejections. Heartbreaks. Our marriage was painstakingly tested. There are so many details and heartbreaking stories I could share, and they will likely be embedded in my blog entries, but as a means of introduction, my nickname began.

After six years of loss, heartache, and sorrow, our first son,

Brady the "Goat" was born. I placed a picture of him as an eight eight-day-old embryo under my pillow and kissed it every night as I waited two excruciatingly long weeks to find out if he decided to nestle comfortably in my belly.

Fortunately, he did. I was pregnant! On June 12, 2010, Brady Brevic entered our world. He was perfect. Scott's twin. Boy, he was feisty, but he was perfect. A bald firecracker with luscious lips and sparkling blue eyes in which I could swim for days.

After doting on him for hours, it was time for the nurse to remove him from our room, so we could finally sleep. (I was in labor for twenty-five hours). Though I didn't sleep, I appreciated the time for Scott and me to digest what had for so long been a dream. Tears welled in our eyes, and our hearts were bursting with happiness and relief. Scott, the proud dad, spent all his time sending photos of our miracle to everyone we knew, and I just observed with joy as Scott transformed into a dad. Proud and madly in love.

As I anxiously awaited Brady's return from the nursery, I questioned how I would know his cry. They all sounded the same. All babies had the same call, right? As baby after baby journeyed down the hall to their proud mamas, I anxiously wanted to be next. I needed to caress his warm skin and smell that delicious baby scent I craved.

It was time. I could sense Brady's presence in my gut. As his cry approached closer, I smiled big. It was perfect. His cry was perfect, but boy, it was also a tad strange. In fact, he sounded like a goat. As I gazed over at Scott, he appeared to have the same inquisitive eyes. He inquired, "Did we have a baby or a goat?" I cackled and almost peed my pants. (I mean, I did just have a baby). The name stuck — Brady was officially crowned, "Goat."

My younger son, Cody, has his own story. A beautiful one but a difficult one as well. Cody will have his own page. His own day.

But as for the title of my blog, that is the story of how it originated. Brady is the senior goat with fairer skin. Cody is the junior goat and with olive skin. As for me, the proud matriarch, I am proudly crowned — the "mom of goats."

# Hand and the Heart

There are many reasons I am excited about my sabbatical. I am anxious to move further along in my academic endeavors, but I am equally, if not more excited, to organize my home. For years, I have watched cabinets and closets filled with junk, and in the back of my mind, I figured I would eventually get to them. I convinced myself that no one sees them anyway. The rest of my house appears neat and organized, so I accepted the clutter in hidden spaces. However, with this time I've been afforded, I can no longer make excuses. They must be done. Organized. No. More. Shoving.

Yesterday, I challenged myself to take on the worst of them all: the guest room closet. It is one of those closets where you shove something in, close it, and hope an avalanche does not transpire the next time it is opened. To motivate myself, I made a refreshing iced tea, collected my phone and Bluetooth speaker, and journeyed up the flight of stairs, and down the hall to the dreaded guest room closet. I stretched like I was embarking on a long hike, smacked myself in the face a few times, and bellowed, "You've got this!"

Since I cannot do anything without music, I perused the selections on my Amazon Prime list, attempting to locate something motivating. The band, Rage Against the Machine, crossed my mind, but then I giggled with embarrassment and reconsidered. Eventually,

I landed on the band, Hand and the Heart. My husband had played them several times before, but it was more of background music for me. I just listened to them to appease Scott. I honestly did not know much about them or their music.

I had no idea the foreshadowing this band would provide as I hesitantly opened the closet, squinting and hoping I wouldn't get bonked on the head with a candle or glass jar residing inside. After all, the monster of a closet held a conglomeration of rubbish: candles, pillows, vases, photos, dried flowers, old yearbooks. It was the epitome of junk — no rhyme or reason. Just somewhere I could place miscellaneous, useless stuff I collected.

Minute by minute, my motivation increased, and I was feeling empowered and energetic. Throwing away junk is cleansing, but I do not do it often enough. Keeping this energy heightened, I hauled the junk off the shelves and was appalled at what I found. I chuckled a bunch at how ridiculous it was that I stored these items for so long. Thankfully, the comic relief armed me with more perseverance, so my chore continued.

I eventually reached the chore I dreaded most: bags and bags of greeting cards I hoarded for years. Many of them were from people who were no longer in my life — distant memories. And as I loaded them onto my bed, I sighed with apprehension. This chore was going to take forever, and I'd only allotted two hours. I had a schedule, and this did not fit into it.

With all the strength I could muster, I chucked the cards onto the bed and took a deep breath. I knew once I started, I would find the stamina to continue. I opened the first one and the next and kept going. Eventually, I realized that since there were so many genres of cards, I would create Post-it Notes, rubber-band them, and put them into categories. Who knew there were so many? They included: birthdays, anniversaries, engagement, wedding, baby shower, congratulations, and sympathy cards for my beloved father-in-law.

Then with shaking hands and trepidation in my heart, I saw a card out of the corner of my eye. It was titled, "Loss of Baby." I cringed and almost threw up in the same breath. My stomach tightened, my heart wrinkled, and my nose stuffed. I was unprepared for this moment. One by one, I opened the cards and grew increasingly sadder.

What I did not mention in my first post was that before Scott and I had our miracle boy, Brady, we lost a girl at nineteen weeks. I had heard her heartbeat a week before, but when we excitedly entered the ultrasound room to learn the gender of our firstborn, there was no heartbeat. She had passed. This traumatic experience was just one example of the disappointment and heartbreak we experienced while trying to have a baby.

The memories from that day are too painful to share but deeply embed in my subconscious. What I accept now after ten years of periodically mourning is I will never forget her. It was my first pregnancy. The first heartbeat I heard. The first kick I felt. Those memories will be with me forever, and she will permanently reside in my heart.

There have been times when I stop in my tracks thinking about that pregnancy. About our baby girl. The times are random and unexpected. (The gynecologist warned me), but time does heal wounds. It truly does. I did not believe it at the time, but time cures. Restores faith. Remedies a broken heart.

Those beautifully written cards warmed my soul. Good friends, family, co-workers, and some unexpected acquaintances authored the cards, and as I read them, I recalled my thoughts when I read them the first time. I was amazed by how many women experienced the loss of a baby. By virtue of a few words, I created a connection with so many women and a lasting bond. For most of them, they will never know it, but they are rooted in my heart. They are members of motherhood with whom I will forever be grateful because they aided in my healing, supported me, and made me feel loved.

As I reached the end of this collection, I had reached down to check a text message. My eyes were still a bit blurry, and my hand had not recovered from the traumatic experience, but like a beacon of light, something immediately caught my eye. Cody! My youngest son. He is my screensaver and at that moment, a lifesaver. Without the loss of my first baby, Cody would not be in this world. Immediately, my heart swelled with gratitude. Thank you, Cody, for that beautiful smile that radiated through my phone. You helped me pause and recognize how incredibly grateful I am for you. Because of you, I acknowledge that life has a funny way of evolving and briefly allowing us to forget about the trauma and heartache we endured.

That moment ironically occurred, but it was perfect. A reminder. A savior. Recognizing I tend to dwell on the negative, I needed you, Cody, to remind me to stop, appreciate, and persevere through this blessed life. So, my hand grasped my phone; I placed a wet kiss smack-dab on his lips, and with a fiery tear, my heart burst. I recognized my blessings and understood their magnitude.

Who knew cleaning a closet would be so powerful? Though I put this chore off for years, I now feel there was a reason. Healing has occurred from that loss, and this task allowed me to recognize it. From one photo, my heart healed. There will forever be a place in my heart for that baby, but onward I go with a steady hand and a grateful heart.

# Head and the Heart

I lead with my heart. My husband leads with his brain. This revelation took me years to understand. When I was sad, I just wanted a hug, or a, "there, there." Nope. Logic. Always logic. Instead of the gentle caress I craved, Scott shared his reasoning. I resented that. I couldn't understand. Why was it so difficult to acknowledge my tears and let me cry? I mean, this happened in the movies all the time — the romance and the gentle arm rub that soothed the pain.

Well, friend, here is why. We are motivated entirely differently. While my heart craves healing his brain needs to understand why — sometimes causing strife. It has presented itself so many times throughout our twenty years together. For example, when I want to redo our kitchen, he considers the effect on our bank account. If I want a new car, in his mind, the boys' college funds are depleting. And when I found out I was pregnant with a second boy, and so badly wanted a baby girl, he made it clear I should be grateful for having two healthy boys. He was right. I was wrong, but friends, I can't help but lead with my heart.

The truth is that this is what makes our marriage work. If I married another heart follower, we would be broke. I would likely cry incessantly, and I honestly would not be the person I am today. My husband has helped me through some awful times in my life, and during these times, his brain interjected and helped me when I needed it most.

Please do not think Scott has no heart. For that matter, I have no brain. It is just years of wisdom that has brought me to this conclusion. Scott loves like none other, but he reserves that love for those who matter most to him. He hurts easily, and when he does, he reconsiders how he presents love to people. I respect that. For years, I have lived to make others happy, sacrificing happiness. Thankfully, Scott reminds me of this, and the older I get, the more I am conscious of the way people treat me and how I respond to them. I am so grateful for him.

Some would say I am sensitive. The truth is I feel too much. Every word. Every action. Every energy goes straight to my heart. Positive or negative, I feel it. Deeply. And sometimes painfully. Every struggle. Every challenge. Every adversity. Straight to the core.

The heart is an interesting and incredibly powerful organ. According to science, it is 5,000 times more powerful than the brain. The heart acts as an emotional conductor and radiates how you are feeling to every cell in the body via the heart's electromagnetic field. This means a person can feel your heart's energy from five to ten feet away. I find this fascinating, and it makes so much sense.

Have you ever worked for someone who is incredibly intelligent, yet cannot seem to lead the company well? Have you ever tried to have a conversation with someone, and you are incredibly intrigued by their intelligence, but you recognize something lacking? Of course! They likely lack or are low in emotional intelligence. They lead with their brain. Not their heart. Do you realize eighty percent of adult success is due to positive energy? Think for a moment. I am sure if you bring a successful person to mind, you will recognize their positive energy and how well others receive them.

I by no means intend to insult anyone or insist that only people who lead with their hearts are worthy of interaction or enjoy success. Of course not. I am married to a brain-leader, and for goodness sake, I am grateful. I need him and his logic, and he is without question, a successful man. My sensitive self requires a balance, and I can't do it alone. I need a beacon and a savior to rescue me when I am completely falling apart. I need logic. I need to be realistic and authentic with myself at the same time. Friends, this is when I need you. I need both sides.

Scott once told me to be careful with whom I am friends. Look out for the saboteurs. The ones who wish me to fail. Those who take comfort in my vulnerability. His wisdom continued by telling me the importance of each friend fulfilling a place and purpose in my heart — faithful friends who look out for me, who cheer for me, and who receive fulfillment from me in return.

Since purpose is the ultimate fuel for our journey in life, I now lead with my brain when determining my friendships. I mean, I don't keep a scorecard, clearly, but my intuition is much stronger than in the past. I look for a shared purpose. Commonalities. But most importantly, powerful and robust connections are paramount.

I read a great quote: "If I get to be myself, I belong. If I must be like you, I fit in." Genuine connections manifest themselves when there is a strong sense of belonging. It is not difficult to detect. We all crave it. But when leading with our brain, we need to recognize the difference. Belonging feels natural. Fitting in feels wrong. Kind of like that feeling you got in high school when you knew you were doing something wrong, but all your friends were doing it. It was wrong. You knew it. Your gut told you it was wrong, but you were attempting to comply. Ugh! I do not miss that feeling.

To compound this notion, I share that I am so intrigued by the Redwood trees. Stay with me for a moment. I saw a documentary recently, and it explained in detail the purpose of the Redwood tree. It symbolizes wellness, safety, wisdom, and communication. I appreciate all that, but what most intrigued me were the trees' roots. They are shallow. For as robust as they are, their grounding mechanisms are not so strong. The reason for this is fascinating. Redwood trees' roots are mainly above ground. They thrive on connections because they spread their limbs wide and far and wrap themselves around each other, and their branches embrace, connect, and support.

In my mind, these trees represent human nature. Though these trees are a safe harbor for animals, provide winter cover from predators, and they are crucial for stabilizing a stable, human-friendly climate, they thrive on connections. Somehow this phenomenon in nature is prolific. From this, I have learned the importance of both the importance of the brain and the heart. Whether it be marriage, friendships, or any other connections, we need them both. The support and comfort. The logic and purpose. We cannot have one without the other. The brain. The heart. Whatever role you play, own it. Flex it. Each part of us contributes to the collective whole and root in a fulfilling relationship.

I leave you with this: Human connections deeply nurture in the field of a shared story. Being vulnerable attracts honesty and honesty attractions connections. Use your heart to clutch your relationships and allow them to expose your vulnerabilities. They are not a sign of weakness. Vulnerability is the most accurate measure of courage and stems from your powerful heart.

# Unsung

Summer has collapsed into fall. The leaves turn color and gracefully fall to the ground. A quiet, peaceful song breaks the leaves' fall, and before long, they combine into piles of crispy, crunchy leaves covering the kelly-green dewy grass. As the weeks go by, the beauty continues to emerge, leaving the landscape with a crust of a brown sugar blanket. Summer is a distant memory as fall has manifested itself into picturesque terrains. Change is here and ready to be embraced.

I respect fall. Fall is not boastful. It recognizes its importance as one of the transitional seasons and plays its role as a time to let things go. Relinquish control. Trust and fall. Fall carries gold in its pocket, and it assumes the part of the unsung hero of the seasons. Nothing new is growing, but, yet fall is so beautiful and carefree.

Fall is my favorite time of year. I love the aromas, the crisp change of air, and the excitement and anticipation of the upcoming holidays. Fall also brings football season. I grew up watching football with my family. On Sundays, we would cover the family room floor with a sea of blankets, and camp there all day. It not only created valuable bonding time, but it fostered a lifetime love of football.

What I did not realize then but it so crystal clear now is the analogy football makes to life. This epiphany hit me at my son's football game one day. Brady is quite athletic. He did not get it from me, and although Scott was a talented athlete, Brady is different. His determined personality coupled with his athletic prowess allows him to thrive at sports.

Anyway, one afternoon, I watched his football game. Brady scored a touchdown, and the crowd erupted with excitement. On their feet. Hollering his name. High-fiving and jumping for joy. It was undoubtedly a huge touchdown. We were playing an incredible team, and this touchdown meant we were likely to win the game. We were all proud, and the team was thrilled.

What gave me pause, however, was how his name was one of the only ones shouted. He was not in this alone. Without his blockers, he could not have gotten to the outside with a clear view of the end zone. Without his center providing him with the ideal snap, Brady would fumble. My joy turned to confusion. I fell back into my chair, and suddenly, the noises around me became ambient. I did not hear a thing. I could not even tell you how the game ended. I needed to ponder. Figure this game of life out before I left that field.

I was lucky to have my writing journal in my purse, so I could capture my thoughts and make some sense of what was jogging through my head. I proceeded by making a list of all the unsung heroes I could evoke and all the parts that made their whole. Without a stage crew or a chorus, the lead role would lose his/ her luster, and a play would be quite lonely and frankly dull. Without a drummer, guitarist, or sound checkers, music would be one-dimensional and empty. Without a sous chef, the head chef would struggle to provide meals for his customer promptly, and the plates' presentations would be dull.

The list caused me to cringe. Life is about teamwork and collaboration and looking out for each other. Getting each other's backs and realizing the importance of working together. We need each other. Kids need each other, and we need to forge these relationships and flex, honor, and celebrate the many amazing talents, strengths, and passions in our children. Most often, they are part of a team. A cohort. A huddle. Though the leaders may be more apparent and obvious, they need their team. They cannot do it alone.

Since our boys started playing sports, my husband and I have worked to cultivate the team mentality in their heads. We remind them often to thank their teammates and to look out for each other. Embrace the huddle and each member in it. After all, the best and most successful teams recognize each other's talents and foster them in a way that creates mutual respect and appreciation. Take a minute to say thank you and give a high-five. Respect that a team is made up of many parts. Be aware of all of them. They all play a role. Big or small, they contribute to the team.

In short, one benefit of getting older is the amount of wisdom and clarity it provides. Ever since I had the epiphany of unsung heroes, I have been more mindful of all the "teams" in life. From carpools to churches, to politics, to the minutia of everyday life, we are all in this together. Pause and recognize the unsung heroes. Thank them for their collaboration and teamwork.

Falling leaves can be so unassuming, but if you have ever observed a leaf slowly descending from a tree, you know its magnificence. Its silent song is robust. Full of humility. That one leaf plays such a critical role in the bountiful harvest of colorful leaves that are waiting patiently for their teammate. Without it, the ground would be a little less bright. Their dance would be unbalanced and our world a little less beautiful.

# Acorn

I have always been intrigued by the acorn. I love its carrying case, its variety of light to dark brown colors, and most intriguingly how abundantly they grow from the sturdy oak tree. What I learned recently about acorns is they are edible but not in their raw form. They can be toxic, and there is a specific process one must take to make them edible.

According to legend, the acorn is a symbol of how hard works pays off over time. Like others grown from a seed, the acorn is nourished by the earth and warmed by the sun to help prepare it to emerge from the mighty oak tree. This process and its symbolism for life have resonated with me.

Reverting to my childhood, I used to glean the sidewalks, collecting as many acorns as possible. My friends and I used to hold contests for who could gather the most, and that contest flourished into many other competitions; the prettiest one, the biggest one, the pointiest one, and many other redeeming qualities of the acorn held court in our contests. We had a blast, and it was such a simple task that epitomized the innocence of our childhoods.

Like many other childhood experiences, I passed along the idea of acorn collections to my children. Since the time they could walk, we would allot time for acorn collections. As typical of my boys, Brady always desired the most redeeming one with the best quality of casing and the best hue in color. Cody, on the other hand, just wanted numbers. How many could he get? Could he beat Brady and me in the collection of them?

Then one day, Brady asked me why acorns were important. Why did they exist? He was aware they fed the squirrels, but why are they so abundant in number, and why the heck are they so big? No joke, in that exact moment what seemed the enormous most giant acorn in history bonked me on my head. It hurt. It jolted me and caused me some severe pain.

The boys relished in my pain and were doubled over in laughter as I fell to my knees. After the hysterics subsided, I suggested we finish our acorn collection and return home to learn more about the focus of our newfound hobby.

Within seconds, the Google search was complete, and we were replete with knowledge about the acorn. We learned it is the fruit of the oak tree. It most often contains one seed, and rarely but sometimes two seeds. For full growth, it takes between six and twenty-four months, and we learned that a variety of birds, including jays and pigeons, rely on them as a staple in their diet. Also, some small mammals that feed on acorns are mice, squirrels, and other rodents. After acquiring this knowledge, the boys seemed even more proud of their collection, and they were excited to complete our hobby another day. Once again, ready to turn it into a contest.

To refocus, one might wonder how in the world and why I have been thinking about the acorn. I laugh as I think of my readers wondering what is going on in my brain. Well, here it goes. I most recently was reintroduced to the Alex and Ani bracelets. I have a couple, but I never really wore them. They merely took up space in my jewelry box.

However, my family and I recently visited Jamaica, and in the airport on the way home, I was meandering around, window shopping and passing time as I waited for our flight when a jewelry store caught my eye. Being a huge fan of costume jewelry, I moseyed into the store but with no intention of purchasing anything. However, out of the corner of my eye, I spotted the Alex and Ani bracelets. Knowing how so many women adored them, I chose to investigate their allure.

Within a millisecond, I spotted an acorn bracelet. Knowing my affinity for acorns and the history I have with their intrigue; I was taken aback when I realized there was literature that came with the bracelet. The description read as follows: "Unexpected Blessings—potential. The acorn is a reminder that one small seed of hope has the potential to grow into something mighty. A blessing that is full of possibility with just a bit of nourishment will thrive and prosper. Open your mind, heart, and soul to life's unexpected blessings."

I gulped. Gulped so loudly it caused a woman behind me to ask if I was alright. I emitted a small giggle and politely shared I was okay. However, inside I was not completely fine. I was jolted by a painful memory that had, until this moment, nestled in my subconscious.

As I approached the register in slow motion, everything around me melted into the background. The noise of my family rushing me along, the boarding announcements, and the rolling of bulky suitcases all cascaded into one long, laborious growl. I was alone with my thoughts. As far as I could tell, I was alone in the world at that moment.

I do not recall how I paid, what the cashier requested, or how I exited the store that day because all that resounded in my head was the impact the acorn description left on me.

So here it is — acorns symbolize protection, prosperity, and perseverance. Digest that. Imagine how that tiny seed results in the grandeur of such an austere and mighty oak tree. Coupled together, they represent new beginnings, strength, and durability, and without one, the other could not exist. Even in its darkest moments, the acorn is preparing for wonderment and release from the hardy oak tree.

When my mind became clearer, and the nebulous of my thoughts jolted back to reality, I boarded the plane, and at that moment, I immediately reached for my writer's notebook. I was incredibly grateful I brought it. I needed to reflect on why the acorn symbolism was so painful. What in my subconscious caused such agony? It didn't take long before a painful memory entered the forefront of my mind, and the promise I made with it invited me to reflect.

Though I share how we lost our baby girl in 2009, I left out a considerable part of the story. The effect that loss left on me was much more than emotionally. It took an incredible physical toll, and many don't know that after I had the surgery and had to say goodbye to our girl, I was left septic. I didn't realize it at the time because it would take days for my body to respond to the toxicity the baby left behind, but a few days after my surgery, I became gravely ill. I was rushed to the hospital and given an unknown diagnosis. The doctor shared with my husband they would try to save me, but the level of toxicity would likely take my life.

I don't want to dwell on the pain and suffering, but I do want to share with you the promise I made to myself and why the acorn's description had such a profound impact on me.

About three days into my hospital stay, as my body lay weak and fragile, I recall staring out the window. It was a beautiful day. The sun was shining brightly, and cars bustled around, enjoying the splendor of the quintessential spring day. The scene in my mind was the antithesis of how I was feeling, but I was somehow comforted by its magnitude.

As my eyes grew foggy with an onslaught of emotion, I gulped deeply and shed a small tear. I recall being so envious of those cars. The mundane chores they were likely running, the feverish drive to drop off a child at a sports practice, or piano lessons, or the stress of arriving at an appointment on time all seemed thrilling to me at that moment. I would have given anything to be one of those cars – to participate in an ordinary day — to revel in the beauty of the mundane — to salivate over a Macchiato as I accelerate to drop off a child on time. These visions struck a chord, and it hurt me so excruciatingly.

As the tears began to burn my pillow, I laid back, closed my eyes, and began to sob. I was so angry at myself for not relishing in the simple moments, or for being upset when I was late, or when road rage encompassed my body and turned me into an ugly version of myself. Those simple, humdrum moments sometimes end up prospering into so much more — a small seed to a mighty oak tree so taken for granted.

When I recovered, my body became healthy, and I was ready to leave the hospital and begin my healing process, I made a promise to myself. I would drink in the sun. Take notice of the same tree I saw a thousand times and recognize the beauty in the ordinary. I would happily listen to the chirping of a bird and wonder about the message it is sending.

It is such a beautiful world filled with prosperity and possibilities, but because of the chaos, the fears, the mundane tasks we take for granted, we don't notice. Notice it, absorb it, and allow it to penetrate us to our core.

Unfortunately, that day at the airport I was given a rude awakening. I rescinded my promise because I don't always take notice. I don't relish in the beauty of the world often enough. I don't observe the possibilities of moments that begin with a tiny seed, or if I do, they become a distant memory, and I am back in my noisy, cluttered head. I don't want a traumatic experience to snap me back into shape and reality. Sometimes the most uneventful days hold the most beautiful showcases of opportunities.

My friends, it is time to return to my gratitude journal. I have started and stopped it a million times, and here is my observation. When I am gracious in my day and reflect on the grateful experiences of it, I search for them. I hear the tiny voice inside my head say, "Melissa, this something to be grateful for, so remember it, breathe it in, and when you swallow it, allow it to permeate through your mind and body. These are the moments of prosperity, security, and abundance." Take notice.

My friends, I hope it doesn't take an acorn bonking you in the head to remind you of life's beauty. As one of my favorite singers, Dierks Bentley reminds me, "Some days you're just alive, and some days you're livin." We are graced with one life. One opportunity to live our best version of ourselves, plant many seeds, and watch them grow and prosper. Nourish them. Protect them. Let in the sunshine and watch life blossom.

# Hard Hat

In 1987, I was twelve. Seventh grade. That awful, awkward stage when all goes wrong. Friend drama. Boy drama. Terrible skin. Gawky in all ways: long and lanky, horrifying buckteeth, frizzy hair, and a large zit permanently residing in the center of my nose.

With this detailed image of me in your mind, you're slightly amused, and your nose is a little wrinkled with pain. You are likely feeling sorry for me. Yeah, me too. As an adult, I can scoff at those times, but at that time, life was awful. No amount of L'Oreal Pumping Curls could fix my mane. Noxema cream could not solve my acne problem. A nose job was out of the question, and braces were only on the horizon- not a quick-solution for my loathsome overbite.

In my town, seventh grade resided in high school. Our school consisted of grades seventh-twelfth, so this meant my gawky, blundering-self was mandated to walk down those never-ending hallways embarrassed and painfully ashamed of the way I looked in front of upper-classmen. I knew this was a phase. My mom reminded me often, but that didn't appease me at the time. No outfit seemed right. No makeup could cover the constellations on my face, and somehow, I had to manage walking by the gorgeous high school girls who had already passed that awkward stage and emerged as supermodels. These experiences pained me. It was pure torture.

School began, and September came and went in fleeting moments. I survived. Barely. However, when October arrived, there was darkness looming. Halloween was on the horizon, and I was keenly aware it meant I must select a costume to wear to school.

Once again, the awkward stage cackled in my face. Seventh graders did not trick-or-treat. If they did, it was with a pack of friends who were usually participating in seeking out a love interest. Knowing, however, that the school event was imminent, I considered my options. I had already exhausted the usuals: Princess. Ghost. Cat. Scarecrow. Besides, I was a "cool" seventh-grader. It was an opportunity to gain some positive attention, so I must scrutinize wisely.

As was typical for me, I waited until the last minute. I likely procrastinated because I didn't want to face the reality that nothing was going to work. No chance of enhancing this bumbling, awkward body. Not even with a costume. But it was mandatory. My friends somehow convinced me it would be more embarrassing not to partake in this painstakingly awful day. Thus, I conceded.

Feverishly rummaging through my closet was futile. Nothing seemed appropriate or acceptable. Clothes and shoes littered my room — piles and piles of failure. As I collapsed into the mountain of junk covering my floor, I racked my brain for an answer. None came. Tears began to flow, and my stomach churned with disappointment. Eventually, I pulled myself up from the rubbish, and languishingly descended the stairs to locate my mother. I was hopeful she had an answer. She proceeded to tell me it was my responsibility. I was old enough to make my own decisions. Blah! Blah! Blah! She was right, but that was not what I wanted to hear.

With time running out, I had a brainstorm. It was brilliant. Halloween was the one day I could be in disguise. A chance to conceal my flaws. Imperfections. Awkwardness. Yes! I had it. A construction worker. Bam! Hard hat to tame my hair. Black face-paint to camouflage my acne. A flannel to disguise my gangly body. It was all coming together. Thankfully, we owned all the supplies I needed. The one item missing was construction boots. With the last shred of hope, I considered my brother's closet. Bullseye. He owned a pair, and he permitted me to wear them. However, my brother is 6'3," and I was approximately 5'5" at the time.

It was too late to consider any of the formalities. I could not be late for school. As I gathered my lunch and backpack, I proceeded with trepidation. The shoes were enormous. I could barely walk, and the face paint I haphazardly slapped on my body seemed disproportioned. My once brilliant idea now seemed like a mistake. I had no choice. My mom was beeping the horn. My siblings were screaming at me to get in the car. Forward march. Literally.

My stomach was churning. Not only was I remiss in eating breakfast, but my instincts told me this was not going to be a good day. In seventh grade, not many days are positive ones, but the events of the morning seemed like foreshadowing for the day ahead.

As we pulled up to the front of the high school, I could not spot one friend, a comrade — someone to enter the building with me as solace. Lucky for my brother, he proceeded with his friends because he was a cool sophomore — beyond the awkward phase. Halloween for him meant nothing. Just another day at school. For me, it meant fitting in and not blundering in any way.

Reluctantly, I opened the door. The doomsday music cued. Everything appeared to be in slow-motion. My shoes trudged forward, and with each awkward step, a thumping emitted so loudly, neighboring towns could hear them.

My first path on this journey was past the senior lounge. Complete torture to insist seventh graders must walk past it. Each side of the lounge swam with pretentious seniors. They were like hawks waiting for an opportunity to feed on the lower-classmen prey. I felt vulnerable and next in line for the upper-classmen feeding frenzy.

With a fake and forced smile on my face, I gripped my books tightly, quietly praying I would emerge on the other side unharmed. Approximately ten steps into my stride, my oversized shoelace got caught under my oversized shoe. Just like something you would see in an after-school special or a Saturday morning cartoon, in tortoise-like slow-motion, each of my books, single-filled slipped out of my hands. My body lurched forward. My hard hat catapulted through the air, and down I went. All of me laid out — smack-dab in front of the senior lounge.

Within seconds, a crowd of seniors leaped onto the coveted senior bench and began cackling and pointing at the pathetic sight that lay at their feet. I can still picture their faces doubled over with laughter and slapping each other on the backs with excitement from the entertainment for which I provided. It was a scene. People stopped in their tracks to experience the event of the morning — all at my expense.

Unfortunately, not one of those bystanders helped me or gathered my belongings. Truthfully, I didn't want their help. I would have looked even more pathetic than I already did, and I just wanted to crawl into a hole and emerge a new human. But then, the situation got worse. It didn't seem possible, but it did.

As my teary eyes began to assemble my books and gather any pride I had left, I felt a hand reaching towards mine. Hesitantly, I reached up and reciprocated. However, it was the last person on Earth I wanted to see. A teacher. And by the way, he was dressed in a kilt. I had to wake up because I was experiencing a nightmare. Nope. It was Mr. Sailing. I know he meant well, and he observed how no one came to my rescue, but he was not the beacon of hope I desired.

Eventually, this train wreck cleared. Students moseyed to their homerooms, and I managed to place two feet on the ground. However, there was still a major problem looming. I could not proceed with this day. I was humiliated, mortified, and disgraced. I needed a lifeline — a savior. *Who better to save me than my mom?*

With a shred of hope of liberation, I located thirty-five cents in my backpack to call her from the payphone. My hands were shaking, and my knees felt like Jell-O. As I dialed her number, I squeezed my eyes shut so hard, and I could see stars. I prayed she would save me. When she answered, I almost jumped through the phone. "Mom, please come to my rescue!" As I relayed the story, my voice was quivering, and my eyes filled with puddles.

When I finally reached the end of the horrific tale, my mom breathed profoundly and paused. It seemed like years before she finally spoke. I knew with every quiet passing second that I would not like her retort, so as the words emerged, they talked to me in slow-motion. She explained how this experience was part of life. It builds character and makes you strong.

My beacon of light became dim. Then it was extinguished. I was livid and appalled. It was inexplicable that my mom would not gather what remained of me from this horrible morning. No matter what I said or how hard I cried, her decision was final.

When I finally realized there was no hope left, I requested she brings me clothes, a washcloth, and some appropriately fitting shoes. She would not oblige to that request either. Instead, she told me to retrieve my gym clothes, wash my face, and confidently proceed with my day.

I depressingly hung up the phone, placed my books in my hands, and trudged to my gym locker. I remember the clothes so vividly. The outfit consisted of a long-sleeved, pale-pink sweatshirt, and gray sweatpants paired with Ked sneakers. That garb was my nemesis at the time, and I am quite confident I never wore them again. The memory was too painful. Besides, the outfit had black face-paint smeared on it despite my futile attempt to place it on carefully.

After some time, I emerged from the locker room. A sorry soul but I exited. My face resembled muddy waters from black paint mixed with tears, my hair was a rat's nest since I clearly could not wear the hard hat, and my legs moved quite slowly as I recalled the events of the past hour. However, that day resonates with me so clearly. A valuable lesson was surely learned. No, it wasn't that I should wear shoes my size or that I could have chosen a more appropriate costume. It was quite more than that.

As devastating as the moment seemed that day, it is genuinely a small taste of what life brings. Life is hard and can be embarrassing. Humiliating. Difficult. My hope is I will teach my children to place their hard hats on and take each painful moment as a lesson that builds character and makes them stronger.

As a mom, I know it would be so easy and convenient to save my children. I could pick up their clothes from their floor, clean up their toys, rescue them from the embarrassing and humiliating times. However, what do they learn from that? I am incredibly grateful to my mom (in hindsight) for the lesson she taught me that day— get up off the canvas and problem-solve. Figure it out. (I am working on this btw).

My goal is to truly digest — No, I will not drop off your homework if you forgot it. It is not my homework. No, I will not return home to retrieve your water bottle. I didn't leave it on the counter. These lessons are not easy friends. It kills me. But, just as my mom did for me, I need to condition my boys to be responsible and capable.

I am sure I will be faced with situations when I cave, surrender, and bring them something they mistakenly forgot, but I will try very hard to stand my ground and teach them valuable lessons they will bring them on their journey through life. We all need a hard hat. Life throws curve balls and situations that seem unsolvable, and for sure, some are not. However, for those that are, equip yourself with problem-solving skills necessary for this journey of life. Friends, we can suit up, wash off the dirt, and get back on our feet. That seventh-grader in me has got your back.

# Snakeskin

I hate snakes. Despise them. I can't even look at a picture of one. This fear has perpetuated over the years, but it began in kindergarten when a friend brought a snake in for show and tell. We all sat in a circle as she placed her slithery friend in the center. In slow-motion, that snake made a beeline for my skirt, and it traveled straight up my legs to my stomach.

Within seconds of it reaching me, I evacuated the classroom and shook incessantly for hours. My mom had to retrieve me from school, and from that experience, I have never recovered. It left a permanent scar. The mere memory of it gives me chills and causes me to catapult out of my seat.

There were several experiences over the years that compounded my fear of snakes. Ugh! Like the time two impish children for whom I was babysitting decided to chuck their snake straight for my head. I sprinted home — never to return. Though I wasn't asked to babysit for them again, it was worth the escape and refuge.

These experiences indeed only continued. I will never get over them. Now that I have two boys who adore snakes, I consistently need to remind them not even to consider asking me for one. Thankfully, they have settled for two geckos. Anyway, I recently had an epiphany about snakes, but I will get to that later. For now,

I will discuss bees. Awkward transition but mandatory for the tie I will make later.

When I was about ten, I had a defining moment, but one I did not realize the propensity of until now. I was a tomboy. No dolls. No teatime. Nothing feminine. I wanted to be outside getting dirty, making mud pies, and chasing my friends.

I had one friend with whom I liked to spend the most time. For the sake of her possibly reading this, I will name her Claire. Claire was a bully. At least to me. She ruled me. Whatever she said, I did. No questions asked because I wanted to be her. She was tough, assertive, and athletic — all the qualities I wanted to possess. Though she was only two years older than I was, she represented maturity — an idol in a sense.

One summer day, Claire knocked on my door. Back in 1985, kids did that. It was not a strange phenomenon. We actually knocked on our friends' doors without them thinking it was a stranger or someone threatening. As soon as I saw her through the screen door, my heart raced, my palms began to sweat, and my hopes rose. Was she actually there for me?

I insisted my mom answer the door, so I did not look desperate. Claire asked if I could come out and play. I waited patiently in my kitchen, but slowly and confidently (yet shaking), I approached the door and stated, "Yeah. Sure. I will be right out!" I hoped she did not notice the beads of sweat cascading down my lip from my excitement and surprise.

Once outside, Claire insisted I retrieve my bike from the garage. I obliged. Before long, we were off on our adventure. We traveled about 100 yards when she suddenly stopped. Something caught her eye. I did what she did and stopped, too. With a smirk across her face, she slowly turned towards me and stated, "Bees!"

I was confused. Bees? They are not anomalies. What was going on? She proceeded to dare me to throw a rock at them. They were emerging from a hive, and she thought it would be hysterical if I destroyed it. I knew immediately it was a poor decision, but I had to impress her. I should. I needed her. She was everything to me. Unfortunately, I was not everything to her. It was not apparent at the time, but she was thrilled to observe my demise when the rock landed smack dab in the center, and within seconds, an army of enraged bees heading straight towards me.

Jumping on my bike and feverishly riding it home did nothing. It was like a moment from a cartoon. The bees collected in perfect formation. Hand in hand. Wing to wing. They were coming for me, they were angry, and I would pay.

As I exhaustively headed for my house for a haven, I reluctantly peered behind me. Claire was double-over with laughter, and bees were raging. It was a traumatic scene. As my head rotated forward, I sped faster for home, and once there, I made a beeline for the back door. I quickly noticed my mom chatting with a neighbor, but when she saw my face, her face turned pale, and she knew I was in peril. She sprinted towards me, observed the multitude of bees attacking me, and instantly stripped me down to my underwear. By the way, Claire was nowhere.

Eventually, my mom removed the bees, picking them out of my hair and off my body one by one. Eleven bees stung me that day, which caused my face to swell, my body to ache, and my soul to smash into smithereens. All I could think about was, *How could Claire do this to me?*

What I did not know then, but I am quite conscious of now, is Claire represented the type of person I would consistently "chase" my whole life. It was a pattern. I seemed to be a magnet for those who did not have my best interest in mind, and if someone did not like me, I needed to know why even if it meant tirelessly putting my energy into their approval. This situation represented the epitome of that pattern.

Someone I respect, and trust implicitly once explained to me one of the best ways to categorize the people in my life. Out of the 100% of them, fifty percent like me and fifty percent do not. That applies to everyone. Immediately, I was disheartened. Not everyone liked me? Nope. He continued to explain that of the fifty percent who liked me, twenty-five percent like me for the right reason and twenty-five percent like me for the wrong reason.

My brain rattled, but I continued to listen. Out of the twenty-five percent who do not like me, twenty-five percent do not like me for the right reason, and twenty-five percent do not like me for the wrong reason. It took me a while to conceptualize this, but I did. I wrote down the people in my life who likely belonged in each category and was astounded.

What was painful to recognize was the amount of energy I placed into people like Claire. The people who belonged everywhere else but, in the twenty-five percent, who liked me for the right reason. At forty-three, I finally realize how I must seek out, honor, and respect the right people — people who like me for me and who wish the best for my family and me — my support system.

This percentage revelation brings me back to the snake. On some level, subconsciously I think I do not like snakes for what they represent. They are sneaky, slithery, and just downright creepy, but, when I think about their ability to shed, undergo metamorphosis, and recreate themselves, I realize I respect them. When they are too big for their skin and uncomfortable, they leave that skin behind — gone — a mere past existence of themselves.

The irony is palpable. I despise snakes. Why? Maybe they scare me because until now, I did not know how to shed my skin. My fears. My inability to respect me enough to shed those who do not like me. I love the quote, "What others think of you is none of your business." Stop wasting precious energy. From this quote,

I am reminded to embrace that infallible twenty-five percent and tell them how much they mean to you.

Just like my experience with Claire, I now proceed carefully with whom I trust. Unfortunately, I now recognize only a small percentage of the people in my life genuinely care about me. The rest are just curious about me and sadly may root against me. That is difficult to comprehend.

Claire was one of those curious people. She was merely curious about how stupid I would look when that army of bees emerged. Well, she got her show, but the curtains closed. I now have thicker skin, and I intend to shed it when necessary. I will proceed carefully, pause reflectively, and instead of a rock in hand, I will carry my heart.

# Starved

There is beauty, and there is comfort in getting older. I used to dread turning a new year, but thankfully, life has allowed me to gain wisdom. That wisdom opened my eyes. Getting older means eliminating toxic friends and acquiring new, quality ones. It means awakening and being more intuitive and more present. Getting older means recognizing the need to take care of yourself by exercising and eating well. It means taking a fresh breath or breathing through a difficult time. Most importantly, though, getting older has allowed me to relinquish control.

I am a middle child, and I epitomize all the clichés about birth order. I was rebellious as a child — not a troublemaker, but I always had to have the last word, which meant lots of fights with my mother. We always made up, but those fights were brutal sometimes. Being a middle child meant sometimes being at a loss for where I belonged. I wasn't the baby. Not the oldest. Not sure what I was or what role I was born to play.

Most evidently and most embarrassingly, it meant I needed to be the center of attention. As a child, that meant putting on plays for people, and I yearned for the lead. It meant being the teacher with my play pals serving as my students. And when I was alone, it meant pretending to be a movie star or a rock star, or any role I could play that created attention.

In high school, this thirst for attention meant I required lots and lots of friends. Quality at that point did not matter (though I was lucky enough to have a quality best friend and several other good friends). The power of numbers was paramount. By having lots of friends, it meant I was in the thick of things. I needed and craved tons of friends and a busy social life.

Fortunately, my aspirations came true, and my young, ignorant self, believed my appetite for attention was satiated. However, the one place I could not make it work was in sports. My brother and sister were stellar athletes. I am talking like all-state kind of athletes. Their athleticism was the spotlight of our family, and we experienced the same routine nightly — rush home, quickly scarf-down food, get in the car, drop one of them off or watch one of their games, rush home, rush to bed, and repeat. For the most part, I enjoyed this routine. I saw it as an opportunity to hang with my friends or wear the latest cute outfit I put together. I so painfully wanted what they had. It ate away at me.

I attempted my chance in sports, or at least I thought I did. But, honestly, while my sister and brother relinquished time with their friends to practice their seasonal sport, I gabbed on the phone with friends. I somehow believed this was what fulfilled me. I was so painfully wrong. But I tried. I really tried. I eventually convinced myself I could make the basketball team. I was going to do it. How could I not? I was clearly going to make it. I came from an athletic family, and my dad was a high school basketball coach. I was born from the same parents who bore my sister and brother. I could totally do it. Right? Sure. So, I entered the tryouts confidently. It did not take long before I realized I was not cut out for it. As I write the following words, my heart hurts, my stomach turns, and my eyes fill with tears.

At the tryouts, I sat and waited — so frightened but convinced the outcome would be positive. It was my turn to try a layup. I envisioned what my sister and brother would do, and as I laid my first step on the ground, I knew right away, I was not good. I was not them. My gait was awkward, the ball felt slippery, and my form was pitiful. It went wrong, and the worst was yet to come.

When I finished my painful chance, the coach's daughter, who was assisting her father, turned to me and said, "I am surprised you're so bad since your brother is so good." True story. She said that. I thought I misheard her, but no. She said it. Her words ate at me like a parasite, and from that moment on, I would never try another team sport. Eventually, I ran track, but for me, that wasn't the competitive sport I had in mind, and I am reasonably sure no one considered it a sport.

It was back to the Melissa with whom I connected and was comfortable — not sports, Melissa. Social Melissa. The one who starved for attention. *Side note*: it was years later and filled with more wisdom that I realized this yearn for attention was merely because I was a middle child, not because I really needed attention.

Since I couldn't get it on the basketball court, or from any field for that matter, I returned to focusing on my social life. A place I knew. A place I felt safe. Unfortunately, this place of comfort took a turn for the worse. It was my junior year — a pivotal year. Most of my friends were applying to college, and the excitement of receiving acceptance letters was palpable. My friends and I began making plans of whom we would visit first, where we would attend, and what we would wear on the first day. Would we marry someone we met in college? The dreams continued being drafted each day as the school year proceeded, and we waited for letters in the mail.

In the back of my mind, I knew I should be doing what everyone else was doing. I needed to apply. I needed to get into college. It was the plan. A plan that went up in smoke before my eyes, and it was my fault. Had I not focused so much on friends and calculating how many friends I had, my focus would have remained sharp. But it wasn't. And I suffered.

Senior year came and my senior year went. I was late on all my applications, and for that reason, I was not accepted anywhere. It was time to face the music. I had no plan, and it was my fault. I was vulnerable, weak, and it was now all out of my control.

Control. It was all about power. I had none at this point. As my friends anxiously and excitedly shopped for new bedding, decorations for their dorm room, and posters for their walls, I sat home. Where were these friends now? It wasn't their fault. It was mine. I was alone, sad, and depleted of all control.

I needed to take that control back, and friends, it is about to get raw. Real. Vulnerable. I struggled with whether I should share this super personal experience, but I then realized people appreciate vulnerability. It makes us human, and truthfully, I think it makes people feel better about their weaknesses. We all have them, but most of us stifle them. Like we are afraid to be raw and weak. Well, hopefully, this will make one girl, one mom, one teenager realizes the pain that is associated with that I am about to tell you.

I became anorexic, and it was terrible. I starved literally and figuratively. Lonely and starved. *Side note*: please don't judge. I know people will look at me and wonder if I still am, and that bothers me often, but I cannot be a hypocrite. If I am going to be vulnerable, then I need to go all-in and heed my advice. Some will judge. Others will find strength in wisdom. That alone encourages me to share the weakest point in my life.

I won't go into too many details, but I will share that it was so excruciatingly painful. It hurt everyone. My mom. My family. My friends. Me. I think the most painful part is as an adult, filled with wisdom; I know there are so many more answers than what I did to myself. But, friends, it was all about control. I lacked it, and I was determined to get that control back in any way possible.

I knew I could control every calorie and every morsel of food. I would win in the fight against food. I needed to win something since everything else seemed entirely out of my control.

This painful battle lasted almost five years. To think of the damage it did to my body makes me cringe, but since I have painstakingly worked on focusing on the positives in my adult years, I choose to focus on what it taught me, and the character it helped me build. I have spent almost twenty years now taking care of my body. I run, practice yoga, and I meditate. I currently use control more positively. I nurture myself. Not just my body. I reflect on those years and use them as lessons for those I can teach and those I can help. It is a devastating disease that without treatment, can be fatal.

Please know this: it is challenging to help those who have this mental disease, and those who suffer need to help themselves in a way that suits them. I know my mom felt helpless, and it was excruciatingly painful to watch me deteriorate before her eyes, but she couldn't help. I recognize this now as a mom because I would do anything for my children. I am so sorry, mom.

People who know I suffered from this disease often ask me how I overcame it. My answer is time! Time truly heals. Unfortunately, I spent time in the hospital, missed tons of birthdays and holidays because of my fear of eating, but with time, and truthfully, lots of therapy, I was able to regain control of my brain positively. Regrettably, it also meant I had to watch my parents spend endless hours and sleepless nights crying and pleading for me to eat, but in time, I did it myself. I gained control and have not lost it since.

Years later, I remember reflecting on this challenging time in my life, and I realized it stemmed from so many situations where I felt out of control or insignificant in my family. So, I once cried my eyes out to my mom, asking her if I had a talent. From years of envying my brother and sister and their many skills, I was convinced I had none — not one ability. When I was about twenty-five, I asked her to please share a skill of mine with me. She turned to me, and with tears in her eyes, she said,

"Missy, your talent is being a good person."

I laughed.

"Um, of course, you say that. I am your child, and clearly, that is what you say when someone has no talent."

However, her comment burrowed in the back of my mind.

I eventually was accepted to college. As it goes, Trenton State College (my first choice and where my brother was a junior) called me the summer of my freshman year and asked me to come in for an interview. The phone call came after I took control of this awful situation and wrote a letter to them about the possibility of interviewing me. I guess I crushed that interview because by the end of the Dean wrote my schedule for my fall semester at community college, so my credits could transfer quickly in the second semester. I finally felt empowered, and maybe my mom was right. Maybe they saw I would be an asset to their school because I was a good person and a hard worker.

It was my chance — my opportunity. I was not going to let my parents down, but more importantly, I refused to let myself down. I never missed a class. I made the Dean's List every semester, and I graduated with honors. I tell you this not to brag, but because of it now evident I had it in me all along. I lost control along the way, but I got it back, and it came back with a vengeance.

As I sit and write this, tears are pouring on my keyboard. My mom was right. Being a good person is a talent and one not everyone embodies. I was literally and figuratively starved for years, but I am grateful. My control has returned in such a beautiful and compelling way. I no longer need attention. At least not from other people. I do things now for me. The "me" who disappeared as a young girl and who suffered from the "middle-child syndrome."

I nourish my body every day with beautiful and quality friendships, positive thoughts, and cherished life lessons that I will continue to share with my readers. If I can help or reach out to one person with this message, then my intention is fulfilled. I want to help. I was born to help. My once starved, and frail body is now comforted with wisdom, and I now realize I didn't need to make the basketball team. I needed to be my own team — one who maintained control and used it positively in all aspects of life.

# Back Nine

In golf, the "back nine" is also known as, "the turn." It is a time when golfers are led back to the clubhouse to rest momentarily, purchase a hot dog or drink, or use the restroom. It is also a time for them to assess their front nine, gauge how to adjust their swing, and set goals for the next nine.

I love the organization in the game of golf. It gives you a half-time — a temporary pause to reflect on adjustments in your game. Maybe just when you are running on fumes, you get a respite. Or perhaps you are so inspired by your success in the first nine holes, the next nine provide motivation and encouragement.

I have been watching golf my whole life. I recall my dad anxiously pouring his coffee and making camp on the couch to watch the prolific golfers of the 1980s: Gary Player, Tom Watson, Arnold Palmer, Jack Nicklaus, and my favorite, Fred Couples. As I watched, I remember feeling a sense of calm. Golf was quiet. Even the announcers spoke in a solemn voice. It never occurred to me how nervous or anxious the players were as they approached the first tee or any hole for that matter.

Throughout all the tournaments, I remember the announcers paying attention to the back nine. It was that break that allowed for a breather before the nerve-wracking next nine holes. Money. Prestige. A green jacket. Whatever it was, the back nine was the beginning of the end. A winner would be declared, and how the golfers performed in the back nine was critical to the final score.

There have been devastating collapses in golf history. In 2015, Dustin Johnson experienced an epic failure when he blew putts for eagle and birdie on the eighteenth hole of the U.S. Open. Johnson entered the back nine at Chambers Bay up two shots. Instead of walking away with his first major win, Johnson is notorious for experiencing one of golf's greatest collapses because of his performance in the back nine.

Similarly, in the 1996 Masters, Greg Norman blew a six-shot lead by the eleventh hole in the final round of the Masters. In all, Norman had five bogeys and two double bogeys to finish his day at seventy-eight. When interviewed, Norman shared he was trying to fix his swing during the back nine, and he managed to psyche himself out in the process.

Just as there are collapses, however, there are also epic comebacks. For example, in 2000, Tiger Woods in the Pebble Beach Pro-Am who was riding a five-tournament win streak, trailed by seven shots at the turn in the final round. Thanks to a showering of birdies, he tied the lead by the sixteenth hole. He then birdied the eighteenth hole to win the event and complete one of the greatest comebacks of all time.

Similarly, in the 2011 Masters, Charles Schwartzel entered the final round four shots off the lead. Thanks to implosion by Rory McIlroy and a few others on the second nine on Sunday, Schwartzel broke away from the pack by rattling off four straight birdies to end his round and win the Masters.

I share these statistics with you because they are the quintessential examples of how a mindset can alter a game. Sure, talent plays a role, but just like Greg Norman shared, our minds can psyche us out and cause utter failure. Our minds can also be an asset. We can change the way we think, modify our thought patterns, and experience greatness if we allow ourselves to control our destinies.

After researching the qualities of successful people, whether they are athletes, business executives, authors, or whatever other dreams one aspires, I was intrigued by how simple they were and how capable I am to possess them. What resonated the most with me, was how critical the analogous back nine was to the success of embodying and executing these skills.

Take challenges as opportunities — quality one. It seems simple enough. Schwartzel did. As he witnessed the collapse of his fellow golfers, he capitalized on it. Stroke by stroke, he maintained a positive perspective and smiled as he slowly took the lead.

As I approach the back nine of grad school, I am losing steam, and I need to embody this exact quality. Through exuding confidence and persevere, I will confront challenges and view them as opportunities. The monotonous article reading, paper creating, and Blackboard responding has become cumbersome and downright exhausting, but I am reminded to find fuel in my empty tank.

With each letter typed, each paper sent, and every response crafted, I am one step closer to receiving the coveted master's degree. I can't stop now. After all, the best view comes from the hardest climb, and as Thomas Jefferson so eloquently stated, "When you reach the end of your rope, tie a knot and hang on tightly." I am gripping so tightly that I have blisters.

Quality two. Always believe better things are coming. New experiences. More meaning. For so many years, I have adopted a negative mindset. I can distinctly remember waking up each morning and consciously asking myself what bad the day would bring. I began my day that way. How could it possibly improve? I set myself up for failure. I was searching for negativity, and it always found me because I allowed it.

I liken this mindset to marriage. Stay with me. We get married, and it is all so incredibly exciting. Wedding. Honeymoon. Purchasing a home. Having kids. We are disillusioned. We think it is all about unicorns and rainbows. It is hard. Marriage is stinking hard. When we are planning the perfect wedding day, the ideal reception, the cute bridesmaid dresses, we are not considering the obstacles. I am not referring to the difficult decision of who to invite, or with whom they should sit, but the real muck and mire.

Like many of my friends with whom I have discussed this topic, we have sometimes pondered, *No one prepared me for this. Why didn't we discuss this? I wanted three kids. You want two. Why didn't you tell me?* Well, because you don't consider that when you are frolicking on the warm sand in Aruba on your honeymoon. Even if you did, when you didn't receive the response you wanted, you thought how you could change his mind.

When it comes to disciplining children, how do you come to a compromise? I am confident this wasn't a hot topic while sipping a Pina Colada poolside. Yet, here we are. Disagreeing. Debating. Years and years of conditioned behaviors from when we were kids is hard to undo. My rules don't match yours because my parents' rules likely won't match your parents' standards.

Well, friends, when I think it can't get harder, there is a beacon of light. That moment when you look at your spouse and think, we *did it!* This hard work has been worth it. Now, I am not disillusioned to think this always works, and life can most certainly throw curveballs, but I speak for myself when I say by adopting the mindset of using hard work and perseverance, better things will be on their way. Patience is key.

Patience and hard work render time to appreciate quality three — be grateful for all you have in your life. As I have aged, I practice gratitude more often. In my younger years, and sometimes even now, I looked at others and was so painfully envious. I want what they have, what they drive. Their house. hair. Their new white kitchen.

A good friend of mine shared a Buddhi "mudita." It means delighting in pleasures in and feeling happy when others are happy. T at times, especially when we are most envious, it is healthy for body and mind to embody that joy and share it often with others. Recognize, too, that others are feeling similarly. There is something you have that they do not.

I have a story to share that is incredibly embarrassing but related to this quality of gratitude and adopting a joyful mindset. In high school, I had a boyfriend who had a good "girl" friend. She was adorable. Cutest clothes. Best hair and skin. Incredibly artistically talented. Bottom line. She had everything I aspired to possess. Well, this goal to attain her qualities reared itself in such an ugly way. I was so jealous, and I felt out of control. As mentioned in the previous chapter, this was one of the many experiences that led to my anorexia.

Um, I didn't marry him. I don't speak to him. What remains, however, are painful memories of pathetic actions to maintain a high school boyfriend and regret wasting so many brain cells on minutia. Yuck! If only I embodied gratitude for the qualities I possessed. Someone probably looked at me in envy. The forty-three-year-old believes that — the sixteen-year-old epitomized insecurity.

Part of the reason envy got the best of me is because of fear, rejection, and disapproval. Quality four of successful people is they see past fear. They recognize that when you stare it in the face, it crumbles. It is powerless and vulnerable. If I had only seen past the trivialities of adolescence, my experiences would have been different, and many of my painful memories would not exist. My grandfather used to say, "most of your fears never happen,"

...hen I reflect on my most frightening times, he was right. If ...y I had listened and believed him.

I wish my grandfather shouted in my hear in high school when I was on the cross-country team. I was not good. No stamina. Not fast enough. But, most importantly, no determination. I was so scared. *What if I run out of breath? What if someone beats me at the finish line? What if my friend beats me?* Well, this fear held on tightly. When it came time for track practice, inevitably, I would fake an illness. An injury. Any excuse not to practice. My coach knew I was lying. I could see it in his eyes. Disappointment. Disgust. I knew it, but I couldn't get past that demon in my head. Fear controlled me.

It makes me so mad now. I run regularly, and when I get to that point that high school Melissa would have stopped, I push harder. Sometimes I can feel tears well in my eyes, knowing I had it in me all along. I am a good runner replete with stamina, speed, and determination. If I had only exited my comfort zone, told off my fearful mind, and believed in myself, I likely could have been quite a talented runner and asset to the team.

*"A river cuts through a rock not because of its power, but because of its perseverance."* — *unknown*

Fear is temporary, but regret is forever. I wish I digested that back in high school and truthfully through most of my adult life so far. Fear is inanimate. Its most significant and most potent nemesis is courage and courage is about navigating uncertainty. That is the core of it. Once soldiering on past the doubt and recognizing the power of that is nestled inside of us, fear crumbles.

Conquering fear segues into the fifth quality of successful people. Those who flourish keep themselves inspired. Using energy and enthusiasm, successful people believe they are invincible when it comes to reaching their goals. They view life as opportunities. They are that flower that busts through the concrete. It is not meant to be there, but it heroically emerges as a sign of dominance. Positive-minded people view that when a door doesn't open, they can build one. In their minds, what first seemed unreasonable and unattainable presents itself as possible and achievable.

I can recall one time in my life where I adopted this positive mentality, but it took an abundance of time. When it came time to have children, as I mentioned, I assumed my story would fall into place the way I wrote it — those three imagined children: two girls and one boy. Oh, and I would be a young mom. All my children would be born before I was thirty. That was the plan. Yeah, that didn't happen. Years and years of trying to conceive seemed like eons. Disappointment after disappointment. Fear of the unknown. Fear of never having a child. What once seemed like the idyllic plan, crashed right in front of me.

After discovering the reason for not conceiving, I had a choice. Give up or buckle up. I chose the latter. My fear translated to strength, and I finally adopted the positive mentality I avoided for so long. I finally decided it was the one time when I refused to back down or falter. I would have children, no matter what it took. After seven years, one devastating loss, hundreds of doctor visits, sleepless nights, and lots of faith, Brady was born. My miracle.

From my experience of having children, I have learned the power and strength I possess. It is so incredibly accurate that we are so much stronger than we think. No one would have convinced me before my experience that I could endure what I did and come out the other side stronger. With two babies. Determined and strong. Reminding myself, when I feel weak, I recall this unbelievable strength I possessed and forward I go. Nothing stands in my way. Yes, it takes reminders all the time to maintain this mindset, but my list of goals is diminishing. I have accomplished many, and I will soldier on to knock them out one by one.

The sixth and final characteristic of successful people and the one I saved for the end on purpose is that successful and positive people live in the present moment. Friends, we cannot allow our past to bother us. We can't rewrite it. It is merely a story. Likewise, the future cannot petrify us. We have this moment — just this one. Tomorrow is uncertain.

We get to decide: is it day one or one day? If we are tired of starting over, we need to stop giving up. Choose today to relish in the beauty. Choose today to stop living in fear. Choose today to be inspired. Choose today to embrace the back nine as an opportunity to live in the moment and persevere. Choose challenges as opportunities. Better things are on their way if we believe in them and do so with gratitude in our hearts and positivity in our minds.

# Grounded

We all have a story. A story that molded who we've become and helps determine our future. Sometimes we want to build a time capsule and go back in time. Take back our regretful actions. Rethink our decisions. Apologize to those we've hurt. But sometimes, we want to return to times in our life. Not to change anything, but to feel things twice. Relive that powerful emotion. Feel the mighty surge of happiness as it runs fervently through our bodies.

I want to return to Sundays in the house in which I grew up and experience the tradition, the memories, and the quality time I spent with my parents and siblings. My parents had a strict procedure on Sundays. These rules were handed down from my mom's parents, and at the time, it felt like I was grounded — a young girl with no clue of the foundation laid for my siblings and me.

Our schedule went as follows: church, followed by Sunday school. Immediately after, we would either retreat to my grandparent's or great Aunt Agnes and Uncle Jake's for coffee and cake. From there, we would return home, enjoy an elaborate home-cooked meal, and sit around the dinner table as a family. Once the meal was complete, my siblings and I would take turns clearing the table and washing and drying dishes. The remainder of the day included completing homework, bickering with my siblings, and tons of activities that I will describe in a bit.

What I realize now is, though our day seemed predominantly religious, there was a pervading theme of family — only my parents, my brother Johnny, and my sister Ali, and me. Just the five of us. Yes, we saw others at church, and clearly, we saw my relatives, but my parents did an exceptional job of ensuring we would maintain the sanctity of family.

I need to explain in detail. As I write these details, I hope to relive just a shred of the love I felt, the emotions I experienced, and the pieces of me that were created all those Sundays at 15 Oak Ave in Midland Park, New Jersey. My home. My "will always be home" retreat.

It began on Saturday night. When all my friends were planning the quintessential sleepover, replete with prank calls, clambering over boys, and late-night chats, I was told I was to remain home because we had church the next morning. My response was always, "No," when my friends asked me for a sleepover. Eventually, they knew my parents' rules, and they stopped asking. Of course, as an adolescent girl, this did not go over well. I am quite confident my parents knew I would someday be grateful for those times, but clearly, no young girl recognizes it at the time. "My parents are the worst," and, "All my other friends are going" are words I am sure I uttered more than once.

Following suit, we awoke on Sunday, dressed in our Sunday best and attended our church service. We sat in the same pew, same row, and the same seats every time. We were like soldiers, and none of us questioned the formation. We just did it. The service began, and we knew the exact routine. The hymns, the prayers, the offering, the benediction. All of it. It never seemed to change, and I enjoyed that because I recall being proud of reciting all the words to the Lord's Prayer and the short choral responses interwoven throughout the morning.

My favorite part, however, was the few minutes before the beginning of the sermon. A familiar tune would permeate the congregation, and like clockwork, my grandmother would remove the coveted Canadian pink mints from her purse. The crinkle of the bag would distract us as it passed from one family member to the next, but we didn't care. It was the perfect distraction, and the moment my siblings and I knew we would have some assistance in making it through the sermon. I can still taste the chalky residue from the pink mint that resembled the color of Pepto Bismol. I am not sure I would opt for one of those mints now, but at the time, they were a savior.

The sermon would continue, and I was likely playing M.A.S.H on the church bulletin, hoping the cute boy, Chris, two rows up would be the winner, and we would live in a mansion in Boca Raton and have five kids. I likely finagled it to work out that way. And when I looked up, if he happened to be looking at me too, I assumed we had telepathic powers, and he was feeling and dreaming the same story.

I am not saying I didn't receive some powerful messages from the sermons. I was just a distracted kid who viewed church in a much different way than I would now. It was a habit. Monotonous — a time to follow the program and do so with a smile and concentration on my face.

As the service concluded, the church bells rang, we shook the hands of fellow churchgoers, and we exited the building, ready for the next step on our Sunday journey. Tea and coffee were next. My grandparents and great aunt and uncle took turns. When it was at my grandparents', we enjoyed homemade, delicious pies my grandmother baked. Though they varied in flavor, chocolate pudding with crushed walnuts and lemon meringue were staples and my favorites.

When it was at my great aunt and uncle's, we stomached Entenmann's stale coffee cakes and store-brand grape soda. Their hearts were in the right place, but their choice of Sunday treats was challenging to digest. Not to mention the pervasive smell of mothballs that blanketed their stuffy, crowded home. Bless their souls. We loved them dearly, but their house was straight out of a horror movie.

Once tea and cake time elapsed, we would venture home. Once again, the routine was the same. My dad would mix up a batch of Bloody Mary's, while my mom began her Sunday chores of ironing and doing laundry. Around noon, The Moody Blues, Eagles, or Queen would loudly fill the walls, and we all knew this preferred music signified the next steps of our Sunday ritual – my mom and dad cooking our midday Sunday feast. They ensured our bellies were nourished and satiated with delicious, mouthwatering, well-rounded meals. My Sunday favorites included beef burgundy, Chicken Milano, and goulash.

When we finally sat down to eat, initially no one spoke. We were all ravenous, and we couldn't get the food down our throats quickly enough. But, when we finally came up for air, the conversations that emerged were incredible. It was a time to blow off steam, share our fears, brainstorm ways to end fights with our friends, or laugh at a corny joke my dad would tell.

Probably the most vivid memory was my dad encouraging us to speak in French. He was a high school French teacher and lived in France for a year, so he knew his stuff. "Passez la beurre" (pass the butter) was standard. Then my brother would make fun of the accent, mess up the pronunciation purposely, and we would all laugh and request him to repeat his silly rendition. Family bonding occurred every minute of that meal.

As we approached the end of the meal, and my mom made her way over to my dad's lap (they were so adorable in love), my siblings and I cringed in the apprehension of the dreaded chore of doing the dishes. We didn't have a dishwasher at the time, and the duty seemed difficult and time-consuming. I am sure we complained and claimed it wasn't our turn, but looking back now, I realize how silly it was to bicker because either way, it had to be done, and there was real family bonding unfolding while the chore occurred.

What transpired next was my most vivid memory. I would retire to my room, slam the door, and warn my siblings to leave me alone. With my one-shouldered *Flashdance* sweatshirt in place, I would stand in front of the mirror, press play, and feverishly dance to "Maniac." Envisioning a full audience in front of me, I would dance so hard, the floors would shake, the walls would echo, and everyone in my house would scream, "Stop!" as I pounded on the floors. Of course, being a rebellious adolescent only meant I did it faster, louder, and more often.

My attention would then turn to the WPLJ top 100 countdowns. Making sure I had a blank tape available; I would place it to "Side A" and be ready for the first song I wanted to record. It was a tedious job. Inevitably the radio host, Casey Casum, would throw in one more word and mess up the beginning of my recording, or the end would come early, and I would have excessive speaking at the end, but I adored this hobby.

At the end of the countdown, I would play it back, sing my heart out, and be psyched to listen to it for the remainder of the day. Of course, I would often run into the issue of the fragile tape twisting, which meant I had to retrieve a pencil, gently place it in the circular hole in the tape and hope it didn't rip, but the effort was worth it. "The Warrior" or "Against All Odds" was at stake, and in those precocious years, I believed every word of every song typified my friendships, boys, and dreams. They were all embedded in those lyrics, and I could not mess up the song.

By the way, while I was singing my lungs out and envisioning the boys who were singing to me, I would be anxiously awaiting their phone calls. Because at the time, there were no cell phones. We didn't always know where our friends were or with whom. We didn't track their every movement. We wondered and imagined, and I must tell you, I think we were better off because of it. Instead of our thumb walking miles as we scrolled through our social media sites, we spent time imagining.

Though our hearts may break a little while we anxiously awaited a phone call that never came, we didn't have to painstakingly experience our friends at a sleepover to which we weren't invited, or a boy we liked out with another girl. Sure, we may have heard about it at school, but we didn't have to witness it on social media and cringe with every detail of the events.

The next part of my day was my favorite. When I was bored, I didn't have a computer or phone to fill my time and distract me. Instead, once I grew tired of dancing and singing, I would pester my brother and sister to have a garage sale. We would charge each other for our belongings, and somehow, we all agreed to it. It is laughable now, but it was quite serious for us then. We steadfastly believed in our items.

As the day began to wind down, I would make my way downstairs and watch one of the football games. My dad and brother had them on all day. I am grateful now because those endless games instilled a love for football, and my husband loves that I will watch with him and know what is going on in the plays, the penalties, and the play-calling. The games, once again, also created time for more family bonding. During this time, we would create a picnic on our family room floor, and this took place because my dad didn't want to miss a play of his coveted Giants, and my brother couldn't take not knowing if the Raiders recovered the fumble or came back from a large deficit. These experiences also stamped happy memories of family and fun.

What happened next is one of the most pleasant family memories. My brother would implore my sister and me to create a menu for him for dinner. Though at times we would emphatically deny him, we most often would oblige and begin crafting the name of our restaurant, the menu items, and the cost of each one. My brother likely overordered and laughed a little while we reluctantly labored to the kitchen. Regardless, this memory remains etched in my mind as an essential ingredient of Sundays in my childhood home.

Yes, there were parts of those days that were not always picture-perfect. I recall many fights with my mom because each of us insisting on the last word. But behind those four walls, we knew we could figure it out. It usually meant that I would write a note with checkboxes as to whether she was "still mad," "kind of mad," or she "forgave me," but the talks that ensued because she sat on my bed and would not leave until we worked it out, those are the ones that I took with me and created the fibers of who I am, the mother I wanted to be, and the ways I would handle conflict in my life.

It comes down to this: I believed being sequestered to my house all day on Sunday meant I was grounded, but I misinterpreted it. Each day of our lives, we make deposits into the memory banks of our children, and my parents did one heck of a time depositing those into mine. Our Sunday family traditions countered the alienation from the rest of the world. That grounding of family. The deep roots that grew deeper each week built the foundation for who I am today. I now wish to return to those times to experience them again because there is no more profound love than family. No better and more satisfying feeling than home.

Now having a family of my own, I will create our own unique traditions. Our own story. One that I hope my boys will look back on with a smile on their face, peace in their heart, and gratitude in their minds because I only hope my children will fondly remember their Sundays with our family. I want them to feel grounded in love, forgiveness, and unconditional love because when the roots are deep, there is no reason to fear being grounded.

# Inscription

On Sunday, January 24, 1982, Super Bowl XVI took place at the Pontiac Silverdome in Pontiac, Michigan. This event marked the first time the Super Bowl took place in a cold-weather city. The 49ers, led by the famed quarterback, Joe Montana, defeated the Cincinnati Bengals twenty-twenty-one. Montana led his team to victory by playing a well-disciplined game that included Montana throwing for 157 yards, rushing for another eighteen, and completing fourteen out of twenty-two passes.

The talented Bill Walsh coached the 49ers. Before his arrival, the 49ers suffered a dismal record of two and fourteen and repeated the same dismal record in his first season as coach. However, motivated and determined, Walsh convinced the entire organization to buy into his philosophy of football, and he vowed to turn around a miserable situation. He also drafted quarterback, Joe Montana, in the third round of the NFL Draft. Under his leadership, the 49ers won Super Bowl championships in 1981, 1984, and 1988. Walsh served as the 49ers head coach for ten years, and during his tenure, he and his coaching staff perfected the style of play known popularly as the "West Coast Offense," and Walsh earned the nickname, "The Genius," for both his innovative play-calling and design.

Though my family and I were not fans of either team, Super Bowl Sunday was a monumental day for us. It meant a giant picnic on our family room floor replete with a smorgasbord of appetizers, a mountain of blankets, and plenty of pom-poms and accessories to assist us in entertaining ourselves. My sister and I would create signs, bedazzle them with glitter, and haphazardly place yardsticks on each end to make them stable enough to hold during game time.

Unfortunately, on this Super Bowl Sunday, I was sick. That awful, fever-filled, achy, miserable kind of suffering. Flu-like. I was devastated, and at age eight, I was incredibly sad I would miss out on the family fun. No, instead, I would be confined to my bed, sleeping in three-hour increments. As I lay there, I could smell the usually delicious aroma of appetizers baking, but dry-heaving thinking of trying to digest them. I tossed and turned, trying to make myself comfortable and shedding an occasional tear because I was missing out on the fun.

Eventually, the game ended, and all that remained of the Super Bowl were dirty dishes, mangled up signs, and tired eyes. My sister and brother sleepily ascended the stairs to bed and peeked in to say goodnight to me. Half-awake, I managed to eke out a laboring, "goodnight," and turned over to continue my slumber.

At some point in the night, my high fever caused me to experience an awful nightmare. I remember it vividly. I recall being part of a church choir, and it was my turn to sing a solo. Paralyzed with fear, I began shaking and sweating. As my reluctant feet drudgingly made it to the altar, I awakened in a startle. Covered in gelatin-like sweat, I immediately felt different. I was beyond the usual sick. Something was wrong. As quickly as I could muster, I descended the stairs to find my parents. As a meek, "mommy" sputtered out of my mouth, I instantly collapsed on the floor like a ragdoll.

The subsequent events are blurry. I recall making it to the bathroom and getting sick, but after that, I can only remember foggy details. I do recollect my parents carried me to the couch, taking my temperature, and shaking with fear. My head was spinning, my thoughts mangled, and my sweaty and feverish body lay limp on the couch. At some point, there must have been a loud commotion (likely from my mom being frightened) because one vivid memory I recall is my brother laying over top of me and pleading, "Missy, please don't die. Don't die." Something was wrong with my brain because, though I couldn't speak, I remember thinking, "Ha! Ha! Johnny, you think I'm dying."

Eventually, my grandparents were called to watch my brother and sister while my parents drove me to the hospital. I will never forget this part. As I lay on my mother's lap on the front seat, I recall half-laughing as we pulled up to the hospital. For some reason, I thought the hospital was a fancy restaurant, and though I couldn't manage to talk, I wanted to ask my parents why we were at a restaurant in the middle of the night, especially since I sported my "Great Muppet Caper" pajamas.

The comedic relief ended abruptly when the multitude of doctors and nurses rushed me into the emergency room and hooked me up to an arsenal of machines, tubes, and ventilators. I will never forget the frightened look on my parents' faces, and I so badly wanted to assure them I was okay, and this was all a joke, but my words were jumbled and struggled to reach my tongue.

Once I was attached to all the necessary machines, the head doctor began asking me questions. They were simple. Rudimentary. Yet, incredibly difficult for me to answer. Demands, such as, "Count to ten" were retorted with, "A, B, C." And when implored to say the alphabet, my fever-induced confusion replied with counting out of order. It was bizarre, scary, and nebulous.

After a battery of tests, the diagnosis shared was a seizure brought on by an unusually high fever. This conclusion resulted in a week-long stay in the hospital and day-after-day a litany of tests was conducted to ensure the fever was the cause of the seizure, and there was no underlying health condition. Thankfully, the doctors assured my petrified parents I would be fine. With a massive sigh of relief, and my parents' faces returning to their usual happy selves, we made camp in Room 227 for our weeklong stay.

The days were monotonous and included nurses taking my vitals, controlled tests, and awful meals from the hospital cafeteria. Day after day, the routine was the same, and I was aching to return home, to my bed, to my friends, and yes, even to school. But, with my young age, and the severity of my reaction to the seizure, the doctors insisted I stay the entire week.

Then one day, I had a visitor. The phone rang, and the operator informed my parents there was someone there to see me. With a quizzical look on my mom's face, she inquired about the name of the visitor. With her smile so big, it could fit a hanger in it, my mom obliged and confirmed the visitor was welcome. When she hung up, I begged my mom to share the name of the visitor, but with a pleasant smirk on her face, she stated, "You'll see!"

Time passed in slow-motion as I waited. Then, with a gingerly tap on the door, my eyes turned and met hers. It was Mrs. Benwell. Elderly and cantankerous Mrs. Benwell. My second-grade teacher.

Mrs. Benwell requires an introduction and background, so my readers understand the magnitude of her visit. She intimidated me. She expected a lot out of us, and she ran a tight ship. I learned this the hard way when I thought it would be funny to burp the ABC's to my friend during a writing lesson. It was abundantly clear disrespect would not be tolerated, and I would never consider being out of line again. In the end, I was grateful for her expectations, but at the time, I was nervous.

The same Mrs. Benwell was standing at my hospital room door. I had no idea she had a sympathetic bone in her body, but I could tell by the look in her eye, she was there out of love.

As conditioned by her, I sat up immediately, folded my hands, and greeted her formally. "Hello, Mrs. Benwell. Thank you for coming."

What happened next will forever be etched in my memory. The brain that just a week ago was blurry, confused and muddled was sharp as a tack when it quickly absorbed this moment. Mrs. Benwell sat next to my bed through the night. Minute by minute, hour by hour, Mrs. Benwell emitted love and affection that I would never have witnessed if it weren't for my seizure. Besides providing me with a poster signed by everyone in my class, she purchased a toy for me from the Candy Striper and placed my order when it was time for dinner. She knew I was weak, and she wanted to help.

Most importantly, however, Mrs. Benwell provided me with a piece of herself. She told story after story about her life, how she became a teacher and many other snippets of information that no one in my second-grade class would learn. I felt blessed, honored, and loved. And when she eventually left, I recall pleading for her to stay. She stamped my heart that day, and I will forever be grateful for her visit.

A few days later, the hospital released me. The nurse placed me in a wheelchair, and many family members greeted me as we made our way to my parents' station wagon. My brother and sister jumped on my lap, surprisingly so excited to see me, and when we finally made it to our house, there were signs to welcome me home. I had never been happier to see my home and my bed.

As I recall, on that Monday, I awoke with a spring in my step, immediately got dressed, sprinted down the stairs, and anxiously waited in the car for my mom and siblings. It took years to pull into Godwin School finally, but when we finally did, I flew out, and only half-said goodbye to my mom. Pushing past the other students, I made it to the door of my classroom and greeted Mrs.

Benwell. For the first time, she smiled, winked, and nodded ever so slightly. It was an unspoken agreement. I would never reveal our secret. It was clear Mrs. Benwell's commitment to her ways were steadfast. Never to be altered. I was okay with that because I got to see her as a human — a loving, caring, and nurturing human. Her secret was safe with me.

I had no idea that Super Bowl Sunday would turn out the way it did. It was a frightening time for my family and me, but if it weren't for that seizure, I would never have experienced the other side of Mrs. Benwell. At forty-three, she still holds a special place in my heart and has made an impact on me for life. She played a critical role in my desire to become a teacher. There are many aspects of Mrs. Benwell's teaching that I chose not to adopt, but the empathy she showed me, the love she exuded, and the kindness of not leaving my bedside, that is beyond what classroom lessons teach. She loved me, and I felt it wholeheartedly.

On Sunday, January 24, 1982, Bill Walsh committed to his team. He rose them from the ashes of devastation and was determined to lead his team to victory. From his coaching convictions to his dedication of long nights watching game films, he was determined, and that 49er team felt it. They wanted to fight for him. To win. To support each other. Coach Bill Walsh was instrumental in this team's passion and perseverance, and it was evident in their success.

Mrs. Benwell did the same for me. Here I sit, thirty-five years later still affected by the commitment she showed me and the dedication she made to me during a challenging time in my life. I believe now that Mrs. Benwell thought that the students who challenged her the most, needed her the most. She was right. I needed her because I struggled in school — not because I wasn't smart, but because I lacked focus. She saw the potential. I believe that was part of the reason she was at the hospital. Mrs. Benwell wanted me to know she believed in me. I felt it. I honestly did, and from that moment on, I worked so incredibly hard to please her. Thank you, Mrs. Benwell. Your inscription is forever in my heart.

# Clutter

For most, home is a place where we feel loved. Safe. A place where there is no judgment. A place where even if we experience a bad day, it can be remedied in the comfort of our own home. Home is a refuge — a location blanketed in comfort and support.

When I decorate my home, creating warmth and comfort is paramount. Copious amounts of battery-operated candles emit a warm glow and create a gentle twinkling warmth in my heart. There are pillows — lots of pillows. These welcoming friends partnered with comfy blankets that line the couches, beds, and chairs throughout my home. Though some are for mere decoration, most are waiting to be hugged and embraced. And when one of us is having a bad day, the walls are replete with heartwarming sayings or quotes that penetrate our hearts and provide guidance in our difficult days.

All these components of my house are intentional. They provide solace and contentment. And when someone enters my home, I am proud of the compliments I receive. Most recognize comfort. Some cannot help themselves but to immediately retreat to the couch, snuggle with a fluffy blanket, or stare in awe while focused on the reflections of the candles.

One of my favorite compliments, however, is when someone comments on the organization of my home. My husband and I both loathe clutter, and we spend many hours canvassing areas of the house that need purging. Garbage night is our favorite. We engage in contests as to who can remove the most clutter or trash from our home. Scott usually wins. Unfortunately, I struggle with removing items of the boys because I just can't let go of things that were their favorites. My husband's typical retort is, "Keep the memories. Lose the trash." I know he is right, so I oblige.

There are some locations in my home, however, that no one sees. These are places where I allow clutter to build. I shove items into them, close the door quickly, and hope the next time I open it, an avalanche doesn't ensue. These clutter zones are in my closets—like the one that stores all my emotional greeting cards. For the most part, no one enters them, so they are my secret. If everyone keeps their hands off those doors, I am safe.

No closet requires more attention than the one that holds my clothes. It is my most despised chore. Knowing it will take a lifetime to clean, when I enter it to retrieve my outfit, I quickly close the door, put it out of my mind, and proceed with my day.

I clean this closet twice a year, and I need to prepare myself for this daunting experience. I have to convince myself of this undertaking, so I require stretching, deep breaths, and constant recitations to myself of, *I think I can. I think I can.*

I recently conjured up the strength to attend to this task. A Venti Starbuck's was a must. My Bluetooth speaker screamed motivating songs, and I gathered several Hefty bags intending to remove all the useless clothing items that have exponentially grown since the last time I cleaned it.

Equipped with motivation and determination, I opened the door. Within seconds, I collapsed to the floor, feeling this painful task was unachievable. With every glance, and in every direction, I saw nothing but clutter. Screaming internally, I reprimanded myself for allowing this disaster to get to this point. If only I put away my clothes when I removed them. If only I placed my shoes where they belonged instead of drop-kicking them at the end of the day. And if only I disposed or donated the ridiculous amount of clothes that accumulated on the racks.

Once I was done punishing myself, I picked myself up from the canvas and drafted a plan. Literally, like a coach drawing up plans for his team, I sat down and drew a blueprint for a newly renovated closet — organized and designed to make me proud. The project consisted of cataloging clothing items according to color, filling containers with accessories, and ordering shoes in succession of seasons. A great plan. An achievable plan. I now found the strength to muster setting it in motion.

As I began removing the hangers from the rails, I started smiling, singing, and rejoicing that the task was underway. Hanger after hanger, I removed each item and considered whether the article makes the cut. It became increasingly tricky while pondering, *what-ifs* and, *well maybe I will need this when.* I demanded I was brutally honest with myself. If I hadn't worn it in a year, it was gone. This debate continued in my head with every meticulously tricky decision.

With no warning, an epiphany stopped me in my tracks. My closet was incredibly analogous to my life. The enlightenment that erupted in my brain made so much sense. Each item in my closet provided a lesson or a sermon of discipline. My closet represented the noise in my head that I can't shut off — the one that caused me insomnia, stress, and anxiety. And when I open the disastrous closet, it causes me the same symptoms. I rush in quickly, retrieve my items, and promptly shut it. Put it out of my mind. No time to remedy. No time to clean it. No time to attend to it or make sense of it.

Instead, more and more clothes end up in piles, and more and more shoes catapult into the black hole on the floor. As disappointing as it feels, the door closes, and temporarily, all the items in it are forgotten. This routine continues daily, and instead of dealing with it, I procrastinate because I rationalize that one sees it. No one knows. No one can judge — only me. My noise is my own.

With this epiphany swimming through my head, I continue with my chore — this time, with a different mindset. My clothes become personified, and I analyze each piece with critical eyes. Not only do I decide whether it stays or goes, but I regulate each article according to what it represents. For example, when I locate that piece that has a stain on it or has a small tear, I reminisce about what event occurred when I was wearing it. Does that tear represent a fun, exhilarating moment, or a stupid mistake I made that caused the injury to the clothing? With that discerning eye, I make my decision.

As I continue along, I learn more and more about myself. When I make the tough decisions, I am proud when I can part ways with an article that at one time brought me great joy. Toxic people in my life is next in line with deep thought and reflection. During some stage in my life, they may have pleased me. Happiness. Friendship. But, as our friendship progressed, maybe it became toxic. Exhausting. No, I do not throw those friends away or donate them to Good Will, but they do cause me concern, and it can be challenging to part ways with them.

Then I locate my classic pieces. The ones that always make the cut in my closet. These represent the faithful, dependable, and trustworthy friendships — those worn-in jeans or that faded sweatshirt, or the neutrally-colored shirt that matches every outfit. I don't mean to diminish the importance of these friendships by saying they "make the cut," but I do become enamored with the mainstays. Just like a classic piece of clothing that matches everything and is reliable, a classic friend remains steadfast and true despite my inadequacies, my mistakes, or my situations in life. These articles of clothing bring me happiness and make me smile a little bigger as I gently place them on their hangers and return them to their location in my closet. And as it smiles back at me, I wink in acknowledgment of its importance and mutual understanding.

My eyes then turn to the dreaded decision. The shirt, dress, or pants that were an impulse buy. The ones my friend convinced me to purchase, even though they were out of my comfort zone. The ones I ogle at but can't seem to place on my body because of my concern of what others might think. I think to myself; *I can't pull that off*! Then those same items of clothing preach at me. "For Pete's sake, wear it! The judges are going to judge anyway. No matter what. It's what they do. Wear them. Own it. You be you and let they can be them. Maybe they are jealous because they don't dare to step out of their comfort zone!" Yes! Preach! Now that is gospel.

At in that moment, I plan the quintessential day to sport that gem of an outfit, which brings me to the next thought to digest. Why do we save that special outfit for that special day? When is that special day? What if it never comes? Maybe by then, the outfit is out of style. My thoughts alter to, *today is a great day to have a great day, and by golly, that outfit is going to make me feel great. I am not saving it, right*? We all have those outfits. The ones where we stare at ourselves in the mirror, and think, d*ang, I look good.* No matter who you are. No matter what your taste, style, or body-type, we know what makes us look good. Create your sunshine. Wear it with a smile and feel confident you chose correctly. Because, friends, the way we dress can affect the way we think, and even sometimes the way people react to us.

Side note: sometimes I pretend I am going on a date with my husband, or even more obnoxiously, I am meeting someone famous, and that vignette of my imagination assists me in choosing a stellar outfit. And um, I am going nowhere but work, but boy do I have a great day. Shh! It is a secret.

This entertainment, difficult choices, and analogies of life continues for hours. My clothing becomes people, thoughts, and sometimes hysterical memes. What it provides me is so cathartic. By snuggling my favorite sweater or chucking a toxic shirt across the room, I am giving therapy for myself and consoling, appeasing, or preaching. It is all-encompassing, and I am quite enlightened.

Eventually, the chore is complete. The clothes are color-coded. The hangers are all going the same direction, and my shoes pair with their partner (because I recall the time I wore two different-colored shoes because it was too dark in my room, and I didn't notice they were different). My accessories display great care, and the floor exhibits intentional lines of vacuuming. Difficult decisions are completed, and the cast-asides have been packed up for Good Will.

Momentarily, I shut the door, fall to the ground, and exhale a sigh of relief. My dreaded chore is complete. Before long, I drift off in thought and reflect on what I learned. Most importantly, I recognize what this chore represented. Clutter got between me and the life I want to live and the choices I want to make, and when those loud noises clutter my head, it is difficult to discern what decisions are best for me. For me alone. For no one else.

When I awaken back to reality, I launch myself off the floor and immediately open my closet. I relish in its beauty and its organization. I caress my favorite articles of clothing and place on my big girl heels because I now feel invincible. Those heels grant me the confidence to dissect my life, my friendships, and the difficult decisions that life throws my way. For the rest of the day, I must open the closet fifty times to savor my project and remind myself of my many accomplishments.

My accomplishments help me to stand a bit taller. Smile a little bigger. Laugh a bit more often. My chest fills with pride, and from these feelings, my determination bolsters. I now canvas the house, searching for more projects. What once seemed daunting and unattainable, now creates a surge of energy and motivation.

Equipped with the confidence of decluttering my life, I decide to declutter the noise in my head. Make choices that provide me with comfort, warmth, and solace and learn how to bring these newfound feelings to my already warm and supportive home. Because what I learned from being both a mom and wife is, when my mind is quiet and decluttered, I am a better wife and a more effective mom. My family deserves those qualities because to them; I am that flickering candle and that warm comfy blanket that they crave to hold and embrace.

# Scaffold

This fall, my family traveled to the Great Wolf Lodge in the Poconos. For those who don't know, it is an indoor water park that is tailored to family fun and creating lasting memories. I heard about it for years, but my kids were always too young to appreciate all the resort's offerings. A few weeks ago, I stumbled upon a Groupon for the Lodge, and it seemed like the perfect opportunity, and since I am on sabbatical, I had the luxury of being flexible with the days we could travel.

We ended up choosing the Monday and Tuesday before Thanksgiving, and our boys were ecstatic. They couldn't believe we would allow them to miss school. We did, and we were all anxious and looking forward to some family bonding time that is rare because of the insanity of all our schedules.

When we pulled up the resort, I felt like we had arrived at Wally World from *Christmas Vacation,* except that the resort was open. Crowds of families were bustling to unload their cars, and kids were stumbling over themselves to get inside this wonderland.

Our boys were practically in the front seat clawing at us to park and unload our caravan of supplies for the weekend. When we grew tired of their impatience, we located a spot. Then, after a painfully long walk and our arms tired from carrying our bags, we approached the door. I peeked inside, and my exhausted body immediately grew taller. My smile grew three times the size, and

I was filled with memories from childhood when I saw Disney World for the first time. I knew in an instant; this trip would include happy times and happy children.

After checking in and placing our wolf ears on our heads, we headed to our "Wolf Den." I have never seen the boys so excited. It brought a tear to my eye. I had felt guilty for not bringing them to Disney yet, but at that moment, this was their Disney World. To add to the splendor, the boys had their own "den," replete with bunk beds and flat-screen television. The excitement in our room was palpable.

After the allure of the den wore off, the boys implored us to venture to the water park. Though my husband and I wanted just to relax, we knew we could only deny them for so long before they would pull us by our arms and legs. So, after making eye contact with my husband, and giving an unspoken agreement, we obliged and with bathing suits on, a bag packed, and two anxious boys beaming with anxious frenzy, we made our way down to the park.

As we entered, the potent smell of chlorine ripped through my nose, and my eyes began to burn, but I was able to ignore these sensations because of the number of beaming children and their loud sounds of happiness that echoed throughout the water park. The boys were ready to become a part of this euphoria, and they encouraged me to do the same.

We found a home base, and before I could open my mouth, the boys sprinted into the wave pool without provocation. For a moment, I soaked in their happiness and watched them as their innocent faces smiled back at me. They were in their glory.

With the boys occupied, I looked around the park, observed all the options it had to offer and scanned the waterslides of various heights, a wave pool, an obstacle course, and lots more. An excellent adventure was surely on the horizon.

I then made a checklist in my head about which rides I could handle, and which ones were way too scary to attempt. I was comfortable with my choices, and my attention turned to which ones the boys would try. I knew the tallest ones weren't an option, but I debated whether they would push their limits or be content with the more age-appropriate ones.

In the middle of this thought, Brady emerged from the water and begged me to ascend to what I considered the "not likely to try, but maybe if I find the courage, that would be my limit" slides. My stomach immediately knotted, my toes clenched, and my teeth began to chatter. Turning my head towards my husband, I knew by the look in his eye that I had no choice. I couldn't let either of them down. Reluctantly, I stood up and began coaching myself to push past my fears and summon some courage.

We approached the slides — tube in hand. Brady exhibited no fear, and I was so proud of his fearlessness as he galloped up the stairs and looked back at me with a smile. I, however, approached the stairs with butterflies flurrying in my belly. With each hesitant step, my fear grew, and my toes clawed the stairs as if I was holding on for dear life. And, of course, there had to be a long line. As I waited on the endless meander, my fear bubbled, and my heart spun a little faster.

When we finally made it to the top, I felt safe. Secure. Ready to go. We placed our bodies in the correct configuration, gripped the handlebars, and gave a "we got this" glance to each other as our tube began its descent. With bellowing screams, we meandered down the tunnel with ferocious water splashing in our faces and ripples of water circling our bottoms. When the end finally came, we high-fived, and we were ready for more.

After several more slides and lots more laughs, we returned to our chairs. We were exploding with excitement and encouraged my husband and Cody to try out all our favorites. Cody immediately clamored, "NO!" He was shaking like a leaf. Gripping onto my husband's biceps, he shot us an evil glance and told us to leave him alone. We did, and we felt terrible because he was petrified.

The day continued much the same way. Cody remained in his comfort zone, swimming in the wave pool, completing the obstacle courses, and shooting hopes with the buddies he made. He seemed happy, and I wasn't going to push him to do something with which he wasn't comfortable, but, at the end of the day, as the lifeguards corralled children out of the pool, I noticed Cody staring at the slides. It was as if he was envisioning himself attempting them. I smiled as I gathered our belongings to return to our room.

The next morning, the routine repeated. No sooner did the boys' eyes open, then did they beg to return to the water park. After about an hour of coercion, we returned. When we located our spot and placed our belongings in a safe place, I noticed Cody turned to my husband and whispered. I was hoping he found the courage to attempt a semi-scary water slide. My husband leaned down, clenched Cody's hand, and with only a little resistance, they were on their way to the entrance of the slides.

I was able to see his little, skinny legs waiting on the see-through stairs, and my heart broke as I recognized his apparent fear. Screaming with encouragement, we made eye contact, and he continued to ascend the stairs. Brady and I then waited by where they would emerge into the pool, and we discussed how we knew Cody would enjoy it once he pushed past his fear. Sure enough, he appeared from the bottom of the slide with a smile so broad it filled the pool. Then, tripping over himself as he exited the pool, he ran to me and hugged me tightly as he relayed his experience.

I returned the hug and reminded him he is much braver than he thinks. With a slight tear in his eye, he began apologizing. I was confused.

"For what?" I inquired.

"Well, mommy. You're just not as strong as daddy. That is why I didn't ask you. I knew his legs wouldn't let me go."

Though I was slightly insulted, I told him I understood. Then, with calm imploration, I assured him I would hold him tightly as well. "Just give me a chance." He must have seen the confidence sparkling in my eye because he gripped my hand tightly, and we were on our way.

By the time we reached the landing to make our descent, Cody had released my hand and confidently grabbed a tube. He was ready to go down alone. Though I was reluctant, I knew this was one of those mom moments where I had to relinquish control.

He made his choice of the orange slide. I chose yellow. Then, as I entered the tube, I shot a glance over to Cody and realized he was not in his tube all the way. Before I could even release one of my legs, Cody fell half-way out of the contraption and began tumbling down the slide. I immediately yelled for an employee, and before I knew it, all the lifeguards were whistling that they had an emergency. I panicked. I almost threw up in my mouth as I hung over the railing in fear as I waited for the lifeguards to rescue him.

What seemed like five minutes was likely only ten seconds, but those ten seconds were long enough to discipline myself for allowing him to go alone, assume he would be fine and think he was ready for this experience. As the barrage of punishments surged through my brain, I watched the bottom of the slide. As if taunting me, Cody emerged in the tube. Happy as a clam. Confident as a bird committing itself to flight.

As I sprinted down the stairs and rushed towards him, I noticed his new-found confidence and grinned. He then grabbed me by the shoulders, and with a dead-serious look on his face, he stated, "Mom. I am fine. It was awesome. You don't know how strong I am. I pulled myself up and totally crushed it." With a chuckle and applause, I embraced him and relayed how proud I was of him for rescuing himself.

That moment gave me pause. As if entering a hypnotic state, I reflected on Cody's experience. He experienced a scaffold of fear to bravery. What once seemed impossible to him became achievable because of his ability to get over his fear. He felt the fear and did it anyway, and his self-confidence allowed him to do what he was afraid to do just minutes earlier.

Snapping back to reality, I had an epiphany. We don't fear the unknown. We fear what we *think* we know about the unknown. If we could only run into fear, stare at it confidently, we would scare fear so much, it would run. Its power would be lost. Its ability to scare us— gone.

With pride in my heart and confidence emitting a bright light, I huddled my family together and announced we would take on the most daunting slide. We would do it together — as a team. They all looked at me quizzically, but their confusion quickly turned to eagerness. They were ready. I was ready.

Though the millions of stairs that lie ahead turned my head and stomach into hysteria, I coached myself every step of the way. I talked to myself, encouraged myself, and convinced myself we would all be okay. Then, as we approached the final flight of stairs, a woman caught my eye. She was a few stairs below me and crippled with fear and paralyzed with apprehension. Her eyes were brick red, tears cascaded down her face, and her knuckles were ghost-white from gripping the railing so tightly.

I so badly wanted to coach her much the way I did myself. Tell her that I understood. Tell her that I was in her place the day before. Fear is no joke. It can take control of your every thought and every move. I wanted to reach down and hug her, but it was clear she had to do this on her own. However, I took that pain and emotions with me.

As my family placed our feet in the slots, gripped the handles, and cascaded down the slide in our four-person bobsled, I tried painstakingly hard to capture each moment of that descent. My glances canvassed each of my family member's faces, and I created a snapshot of their beautiful, exhilarated faces as we meandered to the bottom and hugged with excitement, love, and pride.

When I exited the pool, I looked up and searched for the frightened woman. She was nowhere in sight, so I assumed she was on her way down the tunnel. Sure enough, I heard a bellowing excitement echoing in the slide, and within a few seconds, she emerged with the utmost composure and confidence. I was so proud of her. Though that woman will never know the observations I made on that day, her fear and her reaction to the wait on the stairs became embedded in my brain and my heart forever.

I decided to keep this experience to myself, but it dangled in my brain for the remainder of the trip, and when we finally left the Great Wolf Lodge, the ride home consisted of me reflecting on what I learned from those three memorable and incredible days.

A scaffold of fear was pervasive throughout the trip and among Cody, me, and that stranger. It took small steps and layers to push past our fears, but each step provided confidence to support us in the next endeavor. And when we reached the pinnacle of both the park and the crippling anxiety, we pushed harder. Gained more confidence and recognized how we could not give power to our concerns and doubts. We were in charge. The inanimate fear was powerless when we stared in its ugly face.

When we arrived home, I decided to journal everything I fear in life. Whether it was something from the past or something that currently plagued me, I needed to see them in writing. To stare at them and conjure up the strength to see past them.

As the list took fruition, I could feel my nose stuffing, my eyes watering, and my stomach churning. I was appalled at the laundry list of what I fear. Yes, some were insignificant: snakes, clowns, spiders. But there were other ones I didn't even know existed — life-changing ones.

One by one, I went down that list and made strategies to overcome them. Though I couldn't ensure myself they would never happen, I gave a percentage to their likelihood and realized I wasted so much precious time being scared. Somewhere along the way in life, I lost courage. And I screamed in my head to myself and shouted, *courage doesn't mean you don't get afraid, it simply means I won't let fear stop me!*

When I picked myself up from the canvas after a barrage of angry rants to myself, I began a new list. A list of fears with which I got past. Ones with which I gained strength and survived. For example, if someone had told me a year before about losing my precious first child, I would have fallen to my knees and given up hope, wailed in tears, and kicked and screamed in excruciating pain. Before that devastating experience, my body and mind would never have been strong enough to overcome such a traumatic experience. But I did.

If someone had told me I would experience five years of a painful and overwhelming eating disorder, I would have never believed them. I was strong. Healthy. Why would I do that to my body? Well, I did. Five long years of a debilitating disorder that consumed my every minute of every day. I made it through. I got healthy. I defeated the evil thoughts in my brain. And if someone told me I would survive countless years of ruthless bullying by several groups of girls at several times in my life, I would say I was stronger than that, and I could overcome their intimidation.

By no means am I saying there aren't worse things in life. I know my experiences could be more challenging. But it's what I know. It's where my foundation of confidence took shape. These experiences provided the scaffold to accomplish more essential things in life without being afraid of them.

We aren't born with fear. Fear is learned. We choose. How far will we push ourselves? How much will we allow fear to win the tug of war? Do we face it head-on or ignore it so much that it makes us sick?

As a forty-three-year-old, I choose courage. I choose to be on the other side of fear. I choose to look back and watch fear crumble to the ground and dissipate. I choose to ask myself what I could do if I wasn't afraid and navigate through a path of bravery.

My blog was a start. I overcame the fear of wondering what others would think. The fear that others would judge or stigmatize me. *So that's why she's so skinny. She starves herself.* Wrong! I am simply trying to stay healthy and allowing myself to be the person I have always wanted to be — confident and secure.

In short, I had no idea a family getaway would provide such wisdom. No clue that by observing my boys conjure up the confidence to push their limits that I would reflect on my own life. Never would have thought a stranger could ignite a conversation in my head about who I am and who I want to be. But it happened. And from now one, I will believe every event in my life is an opportunity to learn more. To acquire the wisdom to provide strength for myself and my family and to encourage my children. To help them overcome their fears and be a soldier of confidence. Because what I need them to know is everything they desire is on the other side of fear. Push past it, defeat it, dominate it.

# Love Connection

Please tell me you have seen this show. Hosted by Chuck Woolery, it premiered in 1983, and the premise spotlighted either a single man or woman who would watch audition tapes of three potential dates. The three options would discuss what they look for in a significant other. Based on their answers, the contestant would pick one of the three for a date. Then the producers generously paid for the two to go on a private, non-taped date. Between the end of the date and when the couple reappeared on the show, they didn't communicate. The lack of communication made the couple's reappearance on the show more authentic and realistic.

A couple of weeks after the date, the contestant would sit with Woolery in front of a studio audience, and his/her date would be backstage, on a large screen so that the audience could witness the two share details about their experience. Sometimes the couple would venture into explicit details about each other or even insult one another in various ways, but other times the dates were so successful they led to marriage and babies. Either way, at the end of each episode, the audience would vote on the three contestants, and if the audience agreed with the guest's choice, Chuck Woolery offer to pay for a second date. I always hoped this was the case. The love connections made me happy.

The memories of this show make me giggle, smile, and

contemplate them at the same time. Love Connection is the same as modern-day Match.com and other dating sites. The difference is, of course, that Chuck Woolery doesn't pay for the date, and from what I understand, you don't see videos of the prospective love connections on the site, but the end goal is the same. Love. Connection. Possibility.

As I sit here and watch some of the old episodes, I attempt to spot a theme. What makes some of the dates work? What causes their demise? Yes, sometimes it is merely a lack of chemistry or attraction, but my intuition detects something different — connection. I hear it all the time from my friends who are dating or have dated in the past. "There just wasn't a connection." But what does that mean? How do you know you have made a connection with someone?

I am not sure anyone can define a genuine connection. It's ambiguous. Nebulous. Seemingly undefinable. Friends have not indeed been able to identify what makes them compatible with someone or what creates a connection, but they do know when one is made. It is also quite evident when a connection doesn't occur. Sure. It could simply mean not having much in common with someone, or the appearance of the date isn't what they had in mind, but when confronted with what caused the disconnect, confusion strikes them.

I am certainly no expert on dating, but if I could venture a guess, the connection lacks because of a lack of empathy. Lack of understanding is likely not because either of the dates is ice-cold or callous, but maybe in that snippet of time, it is impossible to connect on an intimate level.

The truth is if the initial attraction is not there, the desire to delve deeper probably doesn't exist. I have heard story after story about couples who, years later, reunite from high school and connect because they know each other so well. Other couples connect because of traumatic experiences, or couples who are both divorced and connect because they understand each other and are ready to move forward in life and meet someone who understands their circumstances.

What unites these couples? What causes their deep connection? Often, it is because they empathize with each other. Truly get each other. Feel the pain, grief, or trauma the other experienced and want to assist them in healing. A deep, empathetic connection develops.

Empathy is the ability to understand and share the feelings of another. It is the action of understanding. It is awareness. Being sensitive to and vicariously experiencing the feelings of another. Their thoughts. Their experiences. Their pain. It is putting windows in your walls and allowing others to penetrate your heart and helping to heal it and appease you. Console you. A connection is about two people making the conscious effort of sharing much of themselves.

Relationships are not all about pain and suffering, but as I reflect on the couples I know— the connections of people I know and what made them connect so profoundly, it is meeting dark roads and facing them together. It is understanding each other's shortcomings and evolving and healing together. It is the social-emotional connection that binds their hearts and their souls.

There are other relationships besides the ones whose goals are a lifetime together, and there is other love besides those with a romantic connection. Love presents itself in many forms and so many different capacities. There is love for a friend, love for a child, love for a pet, or love for a student. The list could go on for infinity, and the various types express themselves differently, but the one thread they have in common is the connection of empathy.

Often, the most effective empathizers have experienced

trauma themselves. They have been downtrodden and have likely experienced pain and suffering.

Addiction. Sadness. Depression. Failure. The characteristic they share is they have risen from the ashes, soldiered-on, and made it their life goal to assist others in healing. They have supported them, cared for them, cried with them, and genuinely connected with them. Their empathy is palpable and truly felt by their client, their students, and their patients.

As I reflect on myself and those with whom I connect the best, it is no different. I was a difficult child. Had to have the last word. Had to be the center of attention. Had to be popular. Had to stand out. For what, I am not sure, but I can now embrace my downfalls and use them as a toolbox or resource for those with whom I interact.

From these experiences, however, I have gained the wisdom to grow and help others. As a teacher, it is my responsibility to educate my students. Education also means sharing my mistakes and regrets and for my students to recognize how I overcame them. I want them to understand the magnitude of how learning from mistakes reaps benefits and makes you a stronger person. Through teaching these lessons, we develop connections.

Over my career, I have shared a plethora of stories with my students. They love them, not only because they're entertaining, but because they usually foster connections. For example, they learned I hated reading. For many of my elementary years, I despised it and did what I could to avoid it. I was the kid who made any possible excuse to get out of reading. I would hide in the corner and pretend to read. I would ask to use the bathroom every day during independent reading. I would pretend to leave my book at home and ask if I could go to the library. I attempted all aversions, and they often worked. Thus, for students who try the same tactics, they instantly make a connection.

My stories could fill pages and pages and lots of class time, and I am sure if you asked a counselor or doctor or social worker about their stories, they could do the same. We all want to connect. We want others to soothe us. We want them to be willing to listen. Empathy is a choice. A vulnerable choice and likely one that not everyone chooses to embrace, but at our core, the truth is, everyone hurts. Some people hide it better than others and want their hurt to remain secret.

I am not a hider or an introvert. My heart is an open-book, and I probably share too much, but I yearn for those human connections. I know that by sharing my own stories and making others feel comfortable with my carefree spirit and openness, that maybe they too will feel relaxed enough to share themselves.

One of the many stories I share with friends is about the loss of my first baby. It pains me every day, but when that occurred about ten years ago, I was amazed by the number of people who reached out to me, sent cards, or shared a similar story to mine. People I hardly knew shared in my struggle and were willing to share their battles. Colleagues with whom I barely spoke wrote heartfelt letters about their sympathy and their willingness to listen. I will forever be grateful for these unexpected connections and moments of empathy because, like me, they were willing to be vulnerable and share some of their darkest days.

There are also times when people reached out to me, and I wasn't ready or willing to accept empathy. The most devastating example of this was when I suffered from anorexia. At a frail ninety-five pounds, my cheeks sunk it, my bones protruded, and my ghastly-white complexion resembled a ghost. So many people who cared for me attempted to help me, connect with me, or be empathetic, but I wasn't willing to accept it. Thus, there are some situations in which we welcome empathy and comfort, and other times when we need to do it ourselves. Making those decisions as to which we choose isn't always easy, but from what I have learned, inviting others who I trust in my weakest times almost always gives me comfort and solace.

I learned this lesson when I was a teenager when it was too difficult to explain my battles and how my mind wouldn't relent on starving myself. My struggles were so ugly and embarrassing, and not even my mom could shake me out of the war in my brain. What started as people telling me my calves were large in comparison to the rest of my body, resulted in a numbers game of deprivation and starvation, and this dogfight was challenging to explain to others. I refused help, and anyone who attempted to connect with my struggle.

Regrettably, this stubbornness to accept help meant my family would suffer. My mom would cry, my parents would be left confused, and I allowed it all to occur. From 2,000 calories to 1,200 to a mere 300 a day, the battle was mine, and I didn't want any soldiers in my army. My family witnessed me yearning for naps to ignore the demon of hunger in my belly and the aches and pains that wreaked havoc on my body. They watched the dizziness I experienced that sometimes tackled me to the ground. My poor family witnessed it all and were desperate to connect in some way and accept their empathy, but my stubbornness would not allow it.

No matter what they did, they couldn't force me to eat. My mom couldn't persuade me to get help — therapy to cure me. Unfortunately, it also meant I missed out on the experiences of an eighteen-year-old. My mom knew I would regret it, but she most certainly couldn't convince me of it. And for that mom, I am sorry. I can't imagine observing one of my boys suffer as I did. I can't imagine feeling that helpless. That lost.

And for these reasons, friends, I hope there is one reader out there who I am helping. Maybe a colleague, a friend, or perhaps you, my reader. Whatever the case, please know I understand. You want to help. You want your daughter to heal. You want your son to seek help. You want your sister-in-law to confide in you. I am sorry friends, but it may not be possible. They must fight their own battle and do it in their own way. Wait patiently, and eventually, they will accept your help. It must be when they are ready, but it will happen.

My mom used to cry at my feet for me to overcome my battle. To trust her and to hold her hand through this fight. And when my dad had to rush me to the hospital because of my excruciating stomach pains, he wanted me to see the devastation of this disease, but I wouldn't. Couldn't. This disease controlled me. Every ounce of my being and no one could help me overcome it, but eventually, I was desperate for help and connection. The time will come.

Eventually, I defeated it, but I did it on my own. What once consumed my every thought, and every action now lays dormant inside me. It will always be there, but currently, it serves as a reminder that I am stronger than I think, and I have the choice. I choose to be healthy. I choose not to watch my parents suffer. To not watch my family cry and feel helpless. I choose a life filled with beautiful experiences and delicious food. Food that nourishes me and fuels my body. I choose to live.

And from this experience, I also choose to help. As some of you read my words, please know I am here to listen. To empathize and to assist you in any way I can. I know the signs. I recognize the pain. I am entirely aware when someone is suffering from this debilitating disease, and I so badly want to reach out and tell them I understand. But, from my own experience, I know my help is likely not to be received, but my patient heart will wait and be open for connection when the time is right.

I am not ashamed of my experience. As Brene Brown states so eloquently, "if we share our story with someone who responds with empathy and understanding, shame can't survive." Yes, friends, there are those out to hurt you. To make you suffer and struggle. Some smile and feel happy when you are struggling. But those people are likely struggling themselves and filled with shame — shame that controls them and their actions.

Though no one heals themselves by wounding another, some filled with pain will doggedly try to boomerang their pain on you. Their jealousy and their insecurity will rear its ugly head, and it will attempt to defeat you along with it. Just know, these people are in pain. They are screaming for empathy, but they don't know how to find it. Just observe but do not allow it to overtake you because genuine compassion requires you to step outside your own emotions and to view things from the perspective of another person. Don't judge them. Just observe and allow your empathy to feel their pain. In time, they will heal.

In short, I am thankful for the negative experiences in my life. They opened my eyes to the good things of which I wasn't paying attention to before. These experiences developed my character, made me stronger, and most importantly, they allowed me to build love connections among the many important people in my life, as well as with strangers with whom I may connect in the future. For those connections, I won't just listen to your words. I will listen to your tone, watch your body movements, and your facial expressions. I will hear everything you say and everything you don't. We will connect. We will empathize, but most poignantly and powerfully, we will make a love connection filled with empathy and understanding.

# Service

As I mentioned, I had many goals at the beginning of my sabbatical. Many have been met, crossed off, and accomplished. However, besides joining my blogs into a book, there are a couple of goals still lingering, waiting for their turn to disappear.

One of those goals occurred just yesterday, and it is one that has patiently waiting for years. The goal was to run a particular route on specific roads at a precise pace. The thought of it churned my stomach, ached my knees, and caused me to breathe heavily. I attempted it several times before but never saw it through to the end. It has been frustrating, disheartening, and disappointing.

When I awoke yesterday, I decided it was a good day to face it head-on and no matter what, I would finish the "race." These five miles seemed exponentially farther than they were, but because of my hesitation and fear of failing once again, I created a monster out of them. Five miles became a marathon in my head, and they began to control every painful move as I began to prepare for them.

As I grabbed my running clothes and shoes, I began coaching and convincing myself that today was the day. I roared out loud with a motivational speech and then started feverishly completing a jumping jack's regimen with calisthenics as a finale. With every passing second, my motivation grew, and as I propelled myself down the stairs to collect my headphones, I felt ready.

Brandon Flowers, the lead singer of The Killers, was my choice of music. The first song resounded strongly into my eardrums with the words, "Dreams Come True" echoing at a compelling force. No, this wasn't necessarily a dream come true, but the lyrics were motivating enough to release myself from my house and begin the five-mile journey.

The sun shined brightly and acted as a spotlight for the advent of my race. With one foot in front of the other, I began running. It was a brisk pace and one I knew I could not maintain, but it remained in rhythm with the music and with the fake voices of people cheering me on from the sidelines.

I felt strong, determined, and ready. I felt this indeed was the day. About a quarter-mile into the run, I turned the street corner to the next leg of my run, and I encountered a baffling image. A young man somewhere between the ages of eighteen and twenty-one was running with a military backpack strapped to his shoulders and holding what appeared to be at least ten pounds of items stuffed into it. He was pouring sweat and lumbering with every move. His breath was heavy. His legs were full of cement, and his arms grew limp as he painstakingly moved through the cold air.

This moment immediately gave me pause. My eyes grew wider, my heart skipped a beat, and my music seemed to screech to a halt. The first thought I pondered was, *it took every ounce of my being to motivate myself to run five miles, and this man is running with a bag of bricks on his back?* I suddenly felt pathetic and weak, embarrassed, and ashamed.

With a well of tears filling my eyes, I slowly ran past him, making a note of his appearance. Attempting a half-smile, he nodded in affirmation and a courteous notice of a fellow runner scampering along his path. I returned the smile but felt incredibly guilty as I briskly ran by him. From that moment on, I knew I would finish this run. If this soldier can run in that manner, I most certainly could complete five miles with nothing on my back by the brisk wind swimming over my sweaty shirt.

Each mile became increasingly more difficult, but the vision of this man remained in my head. I would not stop. No matter what the pace, I would not stop. When I reached the two-and-a-half-mile turnaround, the sun blinded me, and the wind overtook me. The back nine of this run was going to challenge every bit of me. Again, I convinced myself nothing would stand in my way. I am healthy and strong. My legs and arms work, and my endurance is strong enough to make it to the finish line.

At about mile four, very little remained in my gas tank. I was not confident I could do it, so I began talking out loud and envisioning the military man encouraging me and screaming out motivational phrases that would propel me through the wind and carry me to the finish line of my driveway.

When I approached the final 1000 feet, a gentle tear fell down my face. It was clear. I would accomplish my goal. With every foot that met the pavement, a few more tears cascaded down my face, and by the time I sprinted the last 100 feet, tears multiplied until they became a faucet.

As I made my last step to the finish line, my body doubled over, and I collapsed onto my lawn. By this point, my tears were uncontrollable. They fell because of a conglomeration of so many thoughts. Yes! I was proud. I was darn proud. After all those times of failing, I finally met the finish line with pride. Another goal checked off my list.

But those tears mainly collected because my mind couldn't help but think of that soldier. I wondered where he was in his run. *Did he make it to the finish line? Did his legs stay strong? Were his arms stable enough to carry that load to the end?* Then, my thoughts took a completely different turn. Instead of considering that young man's accomplishments in our peaceful and safe town, I pictured him on the battlefield.

As these thoughts penetrated my heart, I made my way up my driveway and slowly entered my home. I stumbled onto the couch and removed my headphones. In complete silence, I bawled. Tears burned down my sweaty face and rolled sadly down my saturated shirt. With blurry eyes, I canvassed my family room. Bright and cheery Christmas decorations met my eyes with joy, and the shiny lights from the tree danced in a merry pirouette as they meandered up and down the tree.

Though these were beautiful visions and made a valiant effort to lift my mood, I couldn't release the soldier from my mind. This young man was probably preparing for battle, and the heavy backpack was likely replicating ammunition or even a fellow soldier. His run was training, and his exhaustion was nothing compared to the fatigue for which he was preparing.

Emotion and compassion for this soldier paralyzed me. While I sat there and soaked in the beautiful decorations and waited for my healthy and strong young boys to get off the bus, his mom was at home, likely crippled with fear. Though I am sure she is incredibly proud of her son, I cannot imagine how scary it is to send your son into battle. The mere thought sends chills down my spine and causes my heart to break.

With a sudden jerk, I stood up and grabbed a pen and paper. I crafted a list of all the services I do, my children participate in, and future projects that we can do as a family. At the top of that list was the kindness Advent calendar I created for my boys. Each day of December, they complete a small act of kindness. They range from sitting next to someone new at school to bringing coloring books to sick children in local hospitals. They have been completing this calendar for approximately four years, and with each year, the acts become increasingly more intricate and helpful.

I am proud of this calendar, and I am proud of the list I created. It ran the gamut of various aspects of life and with multiple people in our lives. As a mom, I am hopeful this will teach my children some humility and integrity, and they will take these lessons with them throughout life, and their small acts will multiply as others observe their actions, and eventually, our world transforms. Ghandi once stated, "The best way to find yourself is to love yourself in the service of others." Thus, this relay race of kindness is sure to resound with others, and they will work for a cause, not for applause.

As I become increasingly happier and proud of the small services my family and I have completed, my attention once again turns to the holidays and the time of year in which we take part. Christmas is a time for family. For gratitude. For love. For happiness. It is time to stop and pause. Recognize the beauty in the decorations and the way the lights dance in happy unison. The way the smells of Christmas cheer permeate through our houses and their aromas meet us with pleasure.

With all this love, beauty, and refreshing scents come traditions, and we relish in them as we take part. They are ours and ours alone. Each one holds a special place in our hearts. Without them, the holidays would seem a little empty and incomplete. They are a part of us, and they create the cloth of family. They are the fabrics of our happiness and joy.

One of my favorite traditions as a kid was the candlelight service at our church on Christmas Eve. No matter how crazy the holidays became or how stressed my parents were leading up to that service, I knew the finale of the sermon meant the lights would dim and each congregation member would receive a candle. I recall such precious moments as each of my family members would tip their torch to the next family member and greet them with a pleasant smile and gentle kiss on their cheek. It was almost as if there was an unspoken, "We did it," as the candle illuminated, and the flame grew taller.

In unison, we would sing, "Silent Night." I recall even as a kid becoming overcome with emotion. I still cry thinking about it. Silent Night. Yes, silent. Calm. These are not standard terms spoken during the holiday season, but in those moments, there was a blanket of warmth, comfort, and silence covering the congregation. We were in it together, and we felt it deep in our hearts. It was incredibly powerful and meaningful.

So, as I sit here and think about events of the past twenty-four hours, I sit in calm reflection. I am reminded of a quote by Hellen Keller, "I am only one, but still I am one. I cannot do everything, but still, I can do something, and because I cannot do everything, I will not refuse to do something I can do." Keller's words resonate with me because no, I cannot run a marathon yet, but I can run five miles. I can do that, and I will.

That young soldier likely feels compelled to fight for our country because he is young and capable. He feels determined to stand up for what he believes, and likely adopts the mentality of the memorable and honorable soldier, Travis Manion, who believes, "if not me, then who?" For this, I am grateful, and I thank you for your service. Because of you, my kids enjoy a beautiful Christmas. Because of you, we can attend church services in peace. And because of you, I will approach daunting tasks differently. I am sure your mom is incredibly proud. I pray for you. Honor you and respect you.

Merry Christmas, everyone. May you enjoy your holiday season with calm and peace and with family and tradition. And for whatever service you take part, look around and relish in its beauty and who is in attendance. Whether it be in a church or in the comfort of your home or that of a loved one, I wish you a silent and calm night filled with love, peace, and family.

# Countdown

New Year's Eve is a unique holiday. Endearingly titled, "Amateur Night" by my husband, it is an event where young kids can stay up way past their bedtime, and teenagers are out past their curfew feeling empowered and mature. For those my age, it is a night where we dread the next day's removal of decorations and are already anticipating the return to work. One commonality among all ages, however, is that the night dedicates itself to being with close friends and family waiting anxiously for the countdown until midnight. At this moment, the brilliant ball drops in Times Square indicating the start of a new year.

As midnight draws near, kids and adults adorn themselves with hats, glittered glasses, noisemakers, and props to indicate it is time to celebrate. Champagne twinkles and bubbles in glasses, loved ones draw closer, and the television turns to the appropriate celebratory channel.

With the joyous sounds of pops, noisemakers, and celebratory chatter permeating the walls, everyone slides into proper position to ensure he or she is near their loved ones when the clock strikes midnight. It is quite a scene — a vignette of happiness and excitement.

This year, my family and I celebrated with my husband's closest friends from childhood. When the time arrived to countdown to the new year, we situated ourselves in position in our friend's house. My husband and I embraced in excitement, my sons stood below us, and we all made eye contact as if to approve being ready.

Once comfortable, I looked around the room, canvassing the eyes of people we loved, witnessing children popping out of their seats, and admiring the bright decorations that completed the scene of celebration. My smile grew large, my heart skipped a beat, and a surge of strong emotion came over me. The moment had arrived, and I was feeling blessed beyond words.

Ten...nine...eight...seven...the moment was drawing closer. Typically, this countdown meant my eyes fixated on the screen, my knees bent, and my hugs were ready for the moment the clock struck midnight. For some reason, I decided on a different approach this year. It was as if time stood still. The words from the television hosts sounded jumbled, almost as if they were in slow motion, and I reached anxiously for my phone. I quickly turned to the video screen and chose to tape the reactions of the many loved ones as they anxiously awaited the new year.

Though this meant I would miss out on the moment myself, I am incredibly grateful for what I observed. To see the delight on the faces of so many in the room was not only heart-warming, but it was a vision of nothing I have witnessed in my life. For some, it appeared they breathed a sigh of relief. Maybe it was a challenging year. One of sorrow or loss. For heartbreak and disappointment. Maybe they wanted to put that year behind them and move forward. For others, their reaction indicated excitement and possibility. Maybe an exciting event would take place in the upcoming year, or a milestone celebrated. For others, myself included, it was a time to wonder. What would the year bring? Would I finally write the book I aspired to write? Would the goals projected ultimately manifest themselves?

No matter what the reactions demonstrated, I knew each member of the house experienced something that was indeed their own. A moment of release. A moment of uniqueness, and a moment that was their minute one of a new year. As Brad Paisley so eloquently stated, this moment was "the first blank page of a 365-page book." Each member of that house received a privilege — the privilege to write their story. Time for the opportunity to place unique words in their book. Individual vignettes of their life. Time for choices to be made and chapters to fill each page of the upcoming year.

When I reached the final moments of my recorded video, my hand shook, and my eyes welled with ponds of emotion. I reached my husband embracing our two boys. Because of his position so close to me, I was able to witness the precious moment so personally. Individually, he bear-hugged them and relayed his love for them. His first words were, "I love you," followed by, "I am proud of you." My ponds became lakes, which lead to rivers of tears. "I am proud of you." These are not common words recited on New Year's, but they seemed perfect at that moment. He was genuinely proud, and the boys received his praise with affirmation and reciprocated pride. It was a precious moment and one I would have missed if I followed my typical New Year's routine.

When the dust settled, confetti dropped to the floor, and each member of the house proceeded with their night, I collapsed on the couch. I watched the video repeatedly, observing a new reaction or a new face each time. It was eye-opening, quite riveting, and I was grateful I captured these moments.

After I was confident I didn't miss anyone on video, I sat alone and pondered. I created a list in my head of all the countdowns that occur in a year: birthdays, wedding days, retirement, holidays, ends of sporting events. The list seemed endless. I then wondered how often people observed the reactions of people when they are near the end of the countdown. Often, we are too caught up with excitement or the noise in our heads to witness the reactions of others, yet it would be so incredible and fulfilling to observe these moments and their variations. It is not unlike watching the background scenes in movies. Most view the main character or main plot, but when zoomed in on a minor character, the scenes develop with much more clarity and detail.

Equipped with this epiphany, I placed a mental note and promised to zoom in on details more often. Thankfully, a moment quickly presented itself. A couple of days after New Year's, my older son had a basketball game. His third-grade travel team participated in a tournament, and they learned they were playing all fourth-grade teams — clearly daunting and frankly frightening for both the players and their parents.

From the moment we entered the gym, it was evident the fourth graders were taller and more skilled than our players. Nerves grew, and emotions rose. Recognizing we had to surrender to the present moment unconditionally, and without reservation, the boys huddled together, put on their game faces, and entered the court equipped with confidence and teamwork.

Almost immediately, we all realized our boys were ready. Moment after moment, our faces dropped as we witnessed the boys hang in and give the fourth graders a run for their money. The boys played well, and the scoreboard indicated nothing but pure competition and excitement. Nothing was more indicative of this than that out of the four games the boys played, two of them ended with nail-biting, ping-pong scoring, and buzzer-beater endings. We were amazed and so incredibly proud of our team.

After one of the games went into overtime and ended in such a tight match-up, I recalled my new revelation, and I made sure I was attentive during the second nail-biter game to observe during the final countdown (cue Europe) of the game. Instead of watching the clock and fixating on the baskets, I scanned the room. Parents from both teams were on the edge of their seats, and all the players clenched their nails into the bench with excitement. It was incredible — pure heightened emotions and natural competition.

When the final seconds ticked, the opposing team stole the ball from one of our players, and I could watch the excitement erase from our parents and players but amplified on the faces of the opposing team. I knew the ending. The emotion of inevitable loss was palpable, and sadness and disappointment washed over our side's faces, yet to witness this transformation was amazing.

Each person handled it differently. Some hung their heads low; some grew upset and wallowed in tears, and some even looked away. After each one experienced their own emotions, we all turned to each other in admiration and pride of our boys. They fought hard and battled tough. As cheesy as it sounds, they were real winners. They did not relent. They did not cower, and they most certainly did not go down without a fight.

I left the gym that night feeling so fulfilled. Not only was I proud of my son, but I was grateful to have witnessed so much more than a basketball game. I observed the raw emotions of players and their parents as they battled on the court. It was incredible, and yet so new to me. Never did I witness the reactions of so many in so little time and little did I realize all this time that I just had not paid attention.

On the ride home, I was quiet. I was curious and silent. For so many years, I focused on my emotions and reactions, so I missed the responses of others. It is analogous to watching a movie or reading a book more than once. Each time, a new observation made, or a question answered, while new revelations take place almost simultaneously. Again, the key is merely paying attention.

A strange event happened yesterday. I was getting ready in my bathroom, and the song, "Praying" by Kesha came on my Bluetooth speaker. For no apparent reason, I began bawling. Like the kind of cry you experience when you're five, and you lost your puppy. It was an uncontrollable cry that shook my body and burned my eyes.

After what felt like an hour of sobbing, I stared at myself in the mirror and out loud stated, "What is your problem?" Instantaneously, I knew. I was paying attention, and I knew the countdown of my sabbatical had begun. The final three weeks presented themselves, and I became utterly aware of it in those bathroom moments. However, what I quickly pinpointed was these were not tears of sadness. They were tears of pride — tears of happiness and tears of accomplishment.

From the moment my sabbatical journey began, I set goals. I dreamed big and wrote a timeline for these goals. Minute by minute, I drew a draft in my head of which ones had been checked off and completed. I was overwhelmed with what I noticed. My list was almost complete except one — to put all my thoughts and blog entries into a book to round-out my journey and compile them into a book. So, friends, the "mom of goats," has reached the end of my journey of blog-writing for now.

It is time to enjoy my last three weeks by taking in every moment, being present, observing the faces of loved ones along the way, and soaking in each second of time and space I have left before returning to work.

So many have asked me if I am apprehensive or upset to return to my job. The answer is, no! I miss my students and colleagues. I miss the fulfillment I receive each day when I leave my school, and I miss crafting new ideas for lesson plans and activities to complete with my students.

What I will miss, however, is the time and space this sabbatical has afforded me. The time, space, and availability it provided for my family. The calm and peaceful mom and wife. I will miss watching my kids step off the bus and greeting me with a smile.

These moments will be sorely missed. For all these moments, I am grateful.

Thus, as my countdown begins, I will observe my reactions. My moments. My vignettes of time. And, on New Year's Eve of next year, I hope I will enjoy the countdown, react with happiness, and look back on my year with joyful reflection.

Thank you for listening and experiencing life with me. I appreciate your support, your kind words, and your willingness to be vulnerable with me. I am forever grateful. Thank you for the connections we made and the joy, love, connections, and empathy that nestle in my heart, soul, and body.

# The Journey Continues

When I first write the title to this post, I wrote, "The Journey Ends." It made sense. I began this blog with the title, "The Journey Begins," so the logical ending was that it ends. But then I paused. I sat back from the keyboard, looked outside, and consumed a large inhale. Given the breadth of stories, experiences, and lessons expressed in the past fifteen weeks, I couldn't make this post a finale. With a large exhale, and an upright stature in front of my keyboard, I deleted "ends" and replaced it with, "continues."

I had no idea where this sabbatical journey would take me. On day one, I felt liberated. The years of yearning for time and space finally presented themselves. I recognized that I was alone. Alone with my thoughts. Alone in my home. Alone with opportunity. I quickly realized I needed to exhale years and years of fears, anxieties, and life lessons that created a permanent home in my subconscious and nestled comfortably in my gut. It wasn't until I began writing that I became keenly aware that these stories needed to spew out of me via words, phrases, quotes, and emotions. My writing became the vehicle of catharsis, and with every post written, I felt lighter, healthier, and more in touch with who I am.

Recently I was watching a cooking show. I was half-listening as I drafted a list of final chores that required my attention before I returned to work. Then something abruptly caught my attention.

A chef was explaining the uniqueness of the strawberry. He relayed how the strawberry is one of the only fruits that proudly displays its seeds on the outside. While most other fruits conceal their seeds and protect themselves with various shields, skins, and peels, the strawberry surrenders itself to vulnerability.

Intrigued by this phenomenon, I researched the strawberry more in-depth. I figured there had to be something profound. Alas! The strawberry is a symbol for Venus, the Goddess of Love because of its heart shape and red color. Medieval stonemasons used to carve strawberry designs on altars around the tops of pillars in churches and cathedrals. The beautiful and delicious strawberry symbolizes purity, decency, and nobility of spirit.

As I scanned the words and digested each perfectly suited word, I relished in its beauty. My smile increased even more substantially when I made the analogy to myself during this meaningful time of my life. For the first time, I became that strawberry and bore my heart and soul to anyone who would listen. Instead of being fearful of what people would think, how they would judge, and what they might say about me, I erupted with personal stories. Stories of struggle. Stories of hope. Stories of love.

Each week as I completed a blog entry, I pressed "send" with apprehension. I would squint my eyes as I gently tapped the key, and my stomach would immediately lurch in fear. But each time this occurred, I was quickly urged to keep writing. Message after message, I was encouraged by friends, family members, and acquaintances to keep writing. Secure connections ensued, and friendships reignited or grew stronger. Friends from high school would reach out and apologize for being unaware of my struggles. Family members would cry with me as we relived some of my journeys. With each one of these connections, my heart swelled, and I inhaled confidence while exhaling doubt.

So now as I make the final preparations, cross off items on

my checklist, and spend my last days alone, I reflect with pride. As Brene Brown reminds me, "You can't get to courage without walking through vulnerability." I did just that. I opened my heart, shared my innermost struggles, and in doing so, I became aware of my strength. For the first time in quite a long time, I recognized the magnitude of trying something even if it scares me. From these experiences, I feel empowered. I remind myself that I cannot fail if I am myself. I like who I am becoming a lot.

In three days, I return to work. A flurry of emotions overtakes my body and mind. I am excited. I am nervous. I am joyful. Motivated by the opportunity to return to the job I love, interact with amazing students, and reconnect to colleagues I have not seen since June excites me.

Most importantly, I return to work with a heightened awareness of myself — the knowledge of who I am, what I love, and how I react to various situations. For the first time, I have learned to breathe. Breathe in the air, as well as precious moments, opportunities, and connections with those I encounter.

For years I have struggled with anxiety, and that monster created stomach problems, reflux, trouble sleeping, and panic attacks. I was on tons of medicines, visited a plethora of doctors, and insisted on further testing to pinpoint the "problem." Friends. The answer is simple. I didn't know how to breathe. I was unaware of the importance of the breath and its impact on my health.

When I think back to all the times at work when I needed to close my door because I needed to sit down and hope my stomach pains went away. All the nights I was scared to go to bed because I knew I wouldn't sleep, which subsequently meant confronting an awful day. The answer is now clear. Inhale. Exhale. Repeat.

When I wake up on Tuesday from a productive night's sleep, I will first breathe. I will continue to inhale confidence. Exhale doubt. I will crush day one and every day after that. Friends, my journey has just begun. My journey is leading to better days, better experiences, stronger friendships, and more positive experiences with everyone with whom I interact. Through these experiences, insertions of joy, connection, love, and empathy will connect me to myself and others, leaving no room for fear, doubt, and anxiety. I feel strong. I am strong because I proceed with purpose, strategy, and motivation.

Thank you, my friends, for following me on my journey and sharing in the story of my life.

Love, the Mom of Goats xoxo

72247507R00068